A KILLING ON
WALL STREET

A KILLING ON WALL STREET

AN INVESTMENT MYSTERY

DERRICK NIEDERMAN

JOHN WILEY & SONS, INC.

New York • Chichester • Weinheim • Brisbane • Singapore • Toronto

Copyright © 2000 by Derrick Niederman. All rights reserved.

Published by John Wiley & Sons, Inc.

Published simultaneously in Canada.

This publication is designed to provide accurate and authoritative information in regard to the subject matter covered. It is sold with the understanding that the publisher is not engaged in rendering professional services. If professional advice or other expert assistance is required, the services of a competent professional person should be sought.

Library of Congress Cataloging-in-Publication Data:

Niederman, Derrick.
    A killing on Wall Street / Derrick Niederman.
        p. cm.
    ISBN 0-471-37458-X (alk. paper)
      1. Stockbrokers—Fiction. 2. Investments—Fiction. 3. New York (N.Y.)—
Fiction. I. Title.
    PS3564.I343 K55 2000
    813'.54—dc21   00-028300

To Rocket and Sam,
trusty sled team

ACKNOWLEDGMENTS

Is it my imagination, or are my acknowledgment lists getting shorter and shorter? Call it a sign of the times. Websites answer the majority of my questions these days, for which I'm every bit as grateful as the people I would have called instead. However, there are many people who helped me with the details found in A *Killing on Wall Street*, and I want to thank them here.

With that in mind, let me tip my cap to Tim Ryan, Colin Widen, Skip Parker, David Provost, Dick Wood, Bob Quist, Jamie Fagan, Mike Salameh, Noelle Sadler, Mark Panarese, Steve Woodsum, Jeff Sawyer, Russell Miller, Denise Selden, Bob Malloy, Miles Slosberg, Hank Ridless, Tim Everitt, Jay Nelson, and Bob Durkee. The manuscript is better for all of your efforts.

A special word of thanks is due to Stephen Maughan, whose real-life "Gumbuster" company formed the prototype for the fictitious "Gumbegone" found toward the end of the book. I wish you and your enterprise the best of luck.

I'd also like to thank all my friends at John Wiley & Sons. It's been a couple of years since Myles Thompson challenged me to write this book, and I hope it's been worth waiting for. Mina Samuels, Jennifer Pincott, Pamela van Giessen, and Claudio Campuzano did a wonderful job of juggling editorial duties. On the production side, I'm grateful for the work of Mary Daniello, with a special nod to Nancy Land and Maryan Malone of Publications Development Company. Collectively, you have saved me from countless faux pas.

My agent, Charles Everitt, fielded my non-stop inquiries with good cheer and nary a complaint. When the process got bogged down, he debogged it. The fact that the book is coming out ahead of schedule is a tribute to his efforts.

I've got just one more acknowledgment to make. Where would I be in this entire process without Peggy? Not very far, that much is for sure. Thanks, P., for being there every step of the way.

DERRICK NIEDERMAN

A KILLING ON
WALL STREET

CHAPTER 1

Would you pay $59.98 a month for a phone that never rang? That's the question Cliff Cavanaugh was asking himself. Never mind that his extra line was programmed to ring like the *Hawaii Five-O* theme song. For now, all he got was "The Sounds of Silence," which was lousy for Cliff but good, in a way, for the Wall Street population as a whole.

Cliff Cavanaugh was fifteen years into the Compound W of investment careers. Everywhere he went, he met up with a big fat wart. He had managed to be one of the few genuinely miserable stockbrokers of the 1980s, all because he hadn't foreseen three wart-like occupational hazards. Wart number one: Building a client base by sucking up to rich people. Wart number two: Realizing that the people whose money you manage want a hand-holder, not a money manager. Wart number three: Discovering that none of your colleagues loses one minute of sleep worrying about warts one and two.

When the mid-'90s arrived, Cliff figured he was ready to put his stockpicking skills to work as an online trader. No more office politics. No more armpit views of Manhattan on the 7:00 A.M. IRT. It was just man and machine this time around, and he was a smash success, at least by the traditional standard of dollars and cents. He had been racking up 40 percent per year on his personal nest egg while incurring next to nothing in brokerage charges.

Alas, that was the problem. Put a buy-and-hold mindset on a day trader's timetable and you get a hybrid with the functionality of a centaur. A really bored centaur. Other traders cured their boredom by shorting Microsoft or buying futures on the Thailand baht, which is to say that losing money quickly does more for your adrenaline than making money slowly. But Cliff knew that his excitement had to come from a different source. A lemonade stand on the autobahn would be an improvement. He was holding out for more.

Cliff's new lot in life began at an investment analysts' luncheon at the Waldorf, in the fall of 1998. He found himself trapped at the same table with August ("Augie") Beauchamp, a part-time portfolio manager and full-time name-dropper at Frontier Associates, a midtown boutique that managed equity portfolios for college endowments and other such institutions. Frontier had been all over the news, and not because of its wizardry with 401(k) plans. Less than a week earlier, its media analyst, Schuyler Dutton, had been beaten to death in his East Side condo. You heard right. Murdered. In cold blood. By some anonymous killer nicknamed "Bamm-Bamm" by *The New York Post*. The crime stood out not only for its locale—a posh bungalow at 89th and Madison—but also because it occurred in the early morning, not exactly prime time in the world of bludgeoneers.

Anyway, when Cliff offered his personal condolences, Beauchamp promptly boasted that he had seen George Soros that very morning, near Rockefeller Center. Amazing. A colleague of his gets snuffed out and all he can think about is sharing sidewalks with his personal hero, Mister Quantum Fund himself. It seems that Soros had appeared on the *Today* show—plugging his book, *The Crisis of Global Capitalism*—at almost precisely the time that Dutton was being murdered some 50 blocks away. That's what Beauchamp said, anyway, at which point Cliff broke into the coldest sweat he'd ever felt outside the hepatitis ward.

It's not that Cliff was impressed that Beauchamp had seen Soros. No, that wasn't it at all. What Cliff knew—and Augie evidently did not—was that George Soros, for all his dabbling in foreign exchange markets, isn't a morning person. He doesn't get up to walk his dog or check what's going on in Zurich, and there's no way in hell he'd get up to appear on *Today* or anything else.

It didn't take more than a quick call to NBC for Cliff to confirm his suspicions. Oh, Soros had been on the show that morning all right, but the segment had been taped the prior afternoon, at the great man's insistence. So much for Augie's pathetic alibi. And too bad for him that the cops had found Schuyler Dutton's TV tuned to NBC, Channel 4, just the way he left it. Case closed.

Cracking the Dutton murder was a nice feather in Cliff's cap. It got him a front-page photo in *The New York Post* ("Famous shamus!"), and even an appearance on the *Today* show. (He asked if they would consider taping the segment the day before. They said no.) The capper was some serious reward money from Frontier Associates, which Cliff considered a payback of sorts for his years of aimless deposits into the Cavanaugh trivia bank. The whole episode got his mind to thinking, "I wonder, could I do this again?" On purpose, no less.

The betting man's answer was an emphatic *No*, but Cliff wasn't so sure. The simple yet largely unknown truth was that with the long bull market had come wealth, with wealth had come greed, with greed had come envy, and with all of those things had come a noticeable spike in the homicide rate among the well-to-do. Investment types still didn't get knocked off very often, mind you, but when they did, the firms loathed the bad publicity. Better still, they had oodles of money at their disposal to hire their own investigator—never mind the allegedly round-the-clock efforts of New York's finest. If they wanted a quick solution, Cliff didn't see why he couldn't be their go-to guy. He had a spotless track record, didn't he? He went so far as to give his fledgling business a name of its own: Moribund Stanley.

Which brings us back to the phone. Fast forward to February 2000. *Hawaii Five-O* was ringing for real. There was no wrong number this time, not even an overzealous telemarketer. This call conveyed word of a victim who was no ordinary victim. The decedent was none other than Kyle Hooperman, portfolio manager extraordinaire, philanthropist, mountain climber, social climber, and charter member of the Westchester Hunting Club.

And one more thing: He was Cliff Cavanaugh's former boss.

▪ ▪ ▪

The case of Kyle Hooperman actually had one similarity to the Dutton case: the victim was found at home. Home for Hooperman was in the suburbs. He lived by himself in a magnificent old stone house on Oneida Road in Rye, New York, tucked in an exclusive residential neighborhood that was literally full of doctors, lawyers, and Indian chiefs. The adjoining streets had names like Seneca, Cayuga, and Onondaga. Nearby was an old-line country club called the Apawamis Club. A few hundred yards in the other direction were Route 95 and the Rye train station.

There were no signs of breaking and entering, so it was assumed that Hooperman knew his assailant. But unlike Dutton, who had been struck from behind, Hooperman was apparently a witness to his last moments on earth. The cause of death was a single shot from a Colt Government Model .380 handgun. The bullet had struck Hooperman just below the heart, perhaps explaining why the killer didn't bother with any additional rounds. One one thousand, two one thousand, and out.

Fittingly, the crime scene suggested that Hooperman was working until the bitter end. On the computer screen in front of his body was a Hoover's research report for a company with the ironic name of 3-D Live. Hooperman didn't even own the stock, which suggested that he was looking to the future even when he had no future. From the coroner's findings, he didn't make it much past 8:00 P.M. on the evening of Thursday, February 24, 2000.

And who might have committed such a dastardly deed? The list of names was the good news. Hooperman had garnered plenty of rivals during his years in the money management field. He was good at what he did, plus he was outspoken, arrogant, and combined the tact of an armadillo with the smugness of a CNBC anchorperson. Anyway, that was the book on him at his longtime employer, Rutherford & Hayes, which, now that Goldman Sachs had gone public, was the last privately owned goliath on Wall Street. Hooperman oversaw much of the retail brokerage operation even as he juggled his own set of a hundred or so clients.

The bad news is that most of these clients figured to be happy. Hooperman was Rutherford & Hayes's answer to King Midas, and he made a mockery of the notion that the best portfolio managers end up managing money for institutions rather than individuals. There was some faint evidence that Hooperman might have lost a step or two, and Cliff found consolation in that. Plus, there was the fact that all it took was one person, pulling the trigger once. But if he was going to sift through a bunch of clients, brokers, portfolio managers, or just plain no-goodniks to find his needle in the haystack, he was going to need some help.

CHAPTER 2

Harrington's was a two-star restaurant that was destined to remain so, barring the emergence of a food critic willing to underweight atmosphere and overweight bratwurst. But the place wasn't exactly hurting for business. It was located two blocks north of the NYU dean's office and was crawling with underage student types with gray sweaters that were too big, and wire-rimmed glasses that were way too small. When Cliff turned from his corner-table perch to look around the room, he couldn't help but feel old. With clientele like this, he could have Eddie Haskell paged and nobody would even notice. Ignoramuses.

As Cliff completed his visual tour and returned to the glass before him, he realized that the generation gap was even worse than he had first feared. Maybe a budding day trader or two could be found in the crowd, but there was surely no one who could possibly relate to his unique life experiences, no one who had seen Black Sabbath live or met Spiro Agnew. *Sigh.* Cliff sat there slurping his third iced-tea-without-ice, which, when ordered in a short glass, looked just like a Jack Daniels, straight up. No one dared disturb the village drunk.

"Hi ya, Cliffie!"

Except Trace, of course.

Trace was Tracy de Grandpre, whose punctuality rivaled Godot's but who otherwise was the perfect partner in crime-solution. By day, she was working on her MFA at NYU's Tisch School, intent on someday making a name for herself in the Broadway theater world. Nature was on her side. She was blessed with one of those names that was impossible to say only once, sort of like Roseanne Roseanadanna or Hohokus, New Jersey. And looking at her just once was also a bit of a challenge. She was wearing a lime angora sweater that seemed to pluck the hazel from her eyes and pull it across the table. She had a thick, yet tamed, mane of reddish auburn hair, shoulder length. It had been two inches or so shorter the last time Cliff saw her. The prior length was perfect. So was this one. And as she took off her coat, Cliff got an ever-so-faint whiff of a perfume he knew but couldn't name. But it was hers, all right. Knowing the Harrington's clientele, it was dollars-to-doughnuts that no one else in the joint was wearing any fragrance whatsoever.

The two had met almost precisely one year before, courtesy of a five-line help-wanted ad in *The New York Review of Books*. Harrington's, the designated meeting spot, was Trace's idea all the way; with its slightly too-bright lights and student infestation, it was probably in her student handbook as the one Manhattan greasy spoon where it was safe enough to hook up with a total stranger.

Where job interviews were concerned, Cliff had taken his cues from Admiral Hyman Rickover. Legend had it that whenever a prospect showed up in Rickover's office, the old admiral made a point of complimenting the prospect on his tie, whether it was wide, narrow, polka-dotted, or paisley. Finally, Rickover would come right out and ask, "Say, could I have that tie?" Those who answered "Yes" managed to lose their neckwear and their job chances, all at once. But Trace didn't have a tie, and Cliff didn't think complimenting her on her silver-and-jade bracelet would have the desired effect. So he had asked her a few simple questions, and she gave a few simple answers:

Question 1: Are you familiar with the term *p/e ratio?*
Answer 1: Sure. You start with *operation* and take off the first and last letters.

Question 2: If you had to pick one adjective to describe yourself, what would it be?

Answer 2: *Disappointed.* I was hoping for a better question.

Cliff hired her on the spot, being careful not to mention that she was the only person who answered his ad.

Trace's role was to finagle information through personal interviews, the likes of which Cliff found himself too shy, too clumsy, or just plain too unresourceful to obtain. It was a simple deal, really. He would pay all of her expenses and provide her with an hourly fee that would make waitressing permanently unattractive. But their precise contractual arrangement was in constant flux. It started with a few requirements from Trace, now legally defined as "Associate."

1. Associate cannot be forced to work on Friday nights.
2. Associate gets to goof on Principal at least once per case.
3. If Principal ever says "You go, girl" to Associate, relationship is dissolved immediately.

After their first case together, Cliff figured he'd better throw in a few provisions of his own:

1a. Principal reserves the right to engage in investment research during the course of the investigation, without being considered a low-grade slacker.
2a. Associate shall confine her written communications to the facts of the case, and shall at no point try and emulate Emily Brontë in her e-mails, as Principal will not be impressed.
3a. Associate should strive to find ways to create interviewing opportunities that do not involve colliding her rented Pontiac Grand Am into the interviewee's unrented Lincoln Town Car.

The contract wasn't exactly the work of Cravath, Swaine, and Moore.

The only truly binding clause was the "error account," which was basically a mechanism for Cliff to dock Trace's pay for any factual mistakes in her reportage. So far, it was nothing more than an idle threat, and things were working out just fine. But the Hooperman case promised to be their biggest challenge yet.

▪ ▪ ▪

"I don't think I've ever heard you say 'portfolio manager' and 'inventive' in the same sentence," Trace laughed.

Cliff said, "Hooperman was different. His rule for investing was to wait for stocks that made everyone else in the office throw up. You've heard of K-I-S-S?"

"As in 'Keep it simple, Stupid'?" Trace asked. Her eyebrows said, "Duh?"

"Well, Hooperman couldn't spell. His idea of K-I-S-S was Kompanies In Serious Shit. In the '80s, he bought Texaco when it filed for bankruptcy, Johnson & Johnson after the Tylenol scare—stuff like that. Every last one of them was a huge success. You know, I think he even bought Union Carbide after it nuked Bhopal."

Cliff took another swig of his fourth iced tea. Trace by now had a Diet Coke. The last time Cliff had come to Harrington's, he'd struck a deal with Sue Ellen, the waitress. If she'd skip the entrees entirely, he'd tip as if they'd had truffles and caviar.

"Actually, my favorite was in the early '90s, when he was managing money for the Calabrese family—you know, the ones who sued Philip Morris when their old man dropped dead after inhaling 40 years' worth of Chesterfields. Well, Hooperman figured the suit had absolutely zero chance, so the week before the decision was announced, he loaded up on out-of-the-money Philip Morris options for the Calabrese account. Sure enough, the company won and the stock popped six points."

"I'm impressed," Trace said.

"Yeah, it was a brilliant stroke, all right. The only problem came when the Calabreses found out where the windfall came from. The idiots didn't realize that buying options doesn't help the company in any way, shape, or form. They sacked Hooperman pronto, and the guy wore disguises to work for about three weeks."

Trace said, "No, I'm impressed that you thought I knew what an out-of-the-money option was."

"Oh, that? Well, let me explain. . . ."

Cliff lowered his voice as he launched into his monologue. Freud would have been proud. It was totally uncool to be out with a gorgeous redhead and be heard discussing stock options, of all things. Except that stock options are the things you get when you join an Internet start-up. He was talking about options *on* common stocks, which was even worse. Cliff felt for a moment that all the tiny wire-rimmed glasses in the room were staring at him as though he was a perverted finance professor. But as long as Trace was listening, he was talking. He pulled out a cocktail napkin from underneath his iced tea and scribbled on the back:

Philip Morris		Mar	June	Sept
26	20	6½	7½	8¾
26	25	1½	3¼	4
26	30	½	1	1½

"Okay, Trace, here's your typical set of option quotations. The number below the company name is the current stock price, let's say 26. The next column of numbers gives what we call the strike prices for the option. The numbers to the right are the prices of the various options, and the months tell you when the options expire."

"Expire? These things die?"

"Faster than a school of guppies," Cliff said. "That's why options are different. But the thing I want you to notice is that the farther out the expiration date, the more you have to pay for the option to buy the damn stock. In other words, right now, you'd have to pay half a dollar per share for the right to buy Philip Morris at 30 any time between now and the third week of March. That's what it means for an option to be out of the money."

Trace said, "Let me get this straight. I can buy Philip Morris directly for $26 a share, but I should be willing to pay someone fifty cents for the right to buy shares at $30? What gives?"

"The reason you might do that is if you think Philip Morris is going to something like $35 a share." Cliff said. "If that happens during the life of your option, then the right to buy the stock at $30 is worth at least $5, which means your option has increased tenfold during a time when the stock itself rose less than 40 percent. Now you're *in* the money instead. It's what's called buying naked call options. Not too shabby, eh?"

"But what if the stock goes to 20 instead?" Trace asked.

"Then the option goes to zero," Cliff said. "It expires worthless. Meanwhile, the stock is down only 20 percent, so the leverage works against you there. But that was the beauty of Hooperman's move. The only way his options were going to expire worthless was if the Calabreses won their suit; but if that were the case, they'd still have come out way ahead. It was one of the best hedge plays I've ever seen. He took an all-or-nothing situation and made it win–win."

"Okay, I get it, but I want to get back to the expiration part," Trace said. "The reason Hooperman was able to score big with Philip Morris options was that he knew when the Calabrese lawsuit decision was going to be made, right?"

"That's right," Cliff said. "Within a few days, anyway."

"But there are options on a whole lot more stocks than just Philip Morris, right?"

Cliff said, "You got it. Say it with more gusto and you could do voiceovers for the CBOE."*

"No, I'm serious. Here's my point. If I bought an option on, I don't know, Exxon—maybe 'cause I thought that oil prices were going up—why in the world should oil prices go up during the life of my option? Who's to say that the option won't expire worthless, and then, four months later, oil prices do go up and the stock follows suit, so I was right all along but I'm left out of the action like an old dishrag?"

"It happens all the time," Cliff said. "The technical description of the phenomenon you just outlined is that you have to be a lucky son of a bitch to make money with naked call options. Like the time Hooperman bought McDonnell Douglas call options, just because he was impressed with the company's cost cutting, or some bullshit like that. Two weeks later, the company was bought out. I'm telling you, the guy had a golden touch."

"I thought you said he was losing his touch," Trace said.

"Well, he might have been; that's all I can really say. Do you remember that lunch where I exposed Augie Beauchamp's bogus alibi?"

"Do I remember? You've only mentioned it about a hundred times," Trace said, with an impish schoolgirl laugh that had to be a one-way ticket to the principal's office.

"Trace, I've only seen you four times in my life," Cliff said.

"Okay, I exaggerated. You've only mentioned the lunch four times then."

"Very funny. But the last time I saw Kyle Hooperman, it was at the same sort of function."

"So we've established what?" Trace asked. "That the man gets hungry at lunchtime?"

"No, the point is that the luncheon was part of a road show for this poor excuse of an Internet company called URLybirds, which

---

* It stands for the Chicago Board Options Exchange, but Trace didn't really care.

Rutherford & Hayes was helping to bring public last fall. The only reason I was there is that I got a call from Linda Greer, an old buddy of mine who happened to be an administrative assistant under Hooperman. The syndicate department wanted her to round up people like me just to fill the empty seats."

"They do the same thing at the Academy Awards," Trace said. "If James Coburn goes to the men's room, someone comes and takes his place for the TV cameras."

Trace's contract still didn't forbid non sequiturs.

Cliff said, "Well, the point is that, according to Linda, Hooperman actually bought shares at the offering."

"You seem surprised."

"Stunned is more like it," Cliff said. "All that URLybirds did was collect URLs—you know, uniform resource locators. Domain names for websites, that's what I meant to say."

"I thought there were people who got rich by owning the rights to those things," Trace said.

"Oh, there are. But it's just not a real business, at least not on the level you'd expect from a public company. I mean, they bragged at the road show about selling names like *wallstreet* and *beastieboys* for big bucks, but it's not as if they had an infinite supply. The only way they could post any earnings is by selling what they owned, but these things aren't annuities. So right away you know that earnings are completely manipulated, because they depend on what the company has decided to unload in any particular quarter. At some point, they'll have nothing left, which is why the stock fell from 20 to 5."

"But why did they go to the trouble of faking their earnings when they knew they'd get caught?" Trace asked.

At last Cliff recognized Trace's perfume: *Naïveté*, by Charles Jourdan.

"Why do companies fake their earnings? Why do dogs lick their genitals? Because they *can*, that's why. Companies have a whole lot more accounting latitude than most people realize. And they get intoxicated by the thrill of going public, and all the money involved. They either deny their problems altogether or figure that they'll solve them before anyone finds out."

Trace said, "But they still need investor types to buy their shares, right? What happened? Was everyone at the lunch intoxicated too?"

Cliff perked up with that one. Wining and dining clients is an age-old strategy, but he'd never considered getting them completely shit-faced before they signed for an offering. Then again, maybe SEC reps carry Breathalyzers.

"Trace, we're talking about 1998 here. Rutherford & Hayes could have floated 15 million shares of dildos.com if they'd felt like it. Anything that had Internet on it was golden." Cliff started shaking his head. "But I still can't believe that URLybirds faked out Kyle Hooperman."

Cliff took a piece of paper from his coat pocket. "Speaking of which, lest I forget the whole reason we're here, Linda Greer gave me the names and numbers of those hapless Hooperman clients that got stuck with URLybirds. There are only a few of them. But just in case they didn't take kindly to the whole experience, I'd like you to check them out."

"And if I'm caught or killed, the IMF secretary will disavow any knowledge of my actions?"

"Something like that," Cliff said. "Good luck."

CHAPTER 3

Cliff sat at his desk, pondering. He did a lot of that. He explained, to anyone who cared, that the tragedy of his life was making the Olympic pondering team in 1980, the year the U.S. boycotted the Summer Games. He had little choice but to make up for lost glory.

This time around, he was pondering something he had picked up from Linda Greer. It didn't come from the recent call about URLybirds. This tidbit dated back to 1997, when Linda had called just dying to relay the latest piece of R&H gossip: Kyle Hooperman had been ordered to dry out at Betty Ford. It passed for a scandal back then.

The move wasn't a big surprise, at least for those who knew Hooperman as a marauding Manhattan moonlighter. In his prime, he had felt a personal obligation to close down the East Side's finest gin mills. The amazing thing was that his carousing never seemed to interfere with his work. But management didn't like the trend. They clamped down and ordered a two-month hiatus. His move to the suburbs came shortly thereafter. Linda said it had made a big difference. Cliff figured Hooperman was the only person who could stay on the wagon while immersed in Rye.

Such pondering aside, Cliff wasn't making much progress on the case. His consolation was that he was in fine investment form. That was his spin, anyway.

Take Wednesday, for example. Cliff's primary accomplishment was *not* buying Eastman Kodak. The choice seemed pretty clear, at least on a long-term theoretical plane. The balance sheet wasn't the problem, and neither was near-term earnings. The truth was that Kodak was a great company. As one of the 30 companies making up the Dow Jones Industrial Average, it was a real blue chip. It had gotten that way because some enterprising fellow named George Eastman had gone out and invented the first commercially viable camera. The Kodak name had become synonymous with quality film processing, a position that had served the company well for over a hundred years. Not bad, in the scheme of things.

But the photo lab of the twenty-first century was going to be a completely different animal. Would it do any good to be the acknowledged leader in film processing if nobody was using film anymore? "Repeat after me," Cliff said to himself: "The market doesn't care if I don't own a digital camera." The fact was that digital processing was taking over, and it was far from clear that Kodak would continue to be the major player. And it's not as if the company could turn on a dime and claim to be the leader in digital processing. Corporations don't abandon their heritage that easily, especially when that heritage is ultra-profitable. So far, Kodak had put millions into digital technology without hitting paydirt. And with Canon, Sony, and a whole laundry list of other folks muscling in, would the profit margins of digital processing be anything like what Kodak was accustomed to? It was entirely possible that Kodak's twenty-first century was going to feature the longest, cruelest water torture ever devised.

None of this was for certain, mind you. Stock market decisions can boil down to educated guesses, and part of the game is deciding which is the educated part and which is the guesswork. If you guess wrong a few times, you're still in the game. Some bright young optimist once claimed that to come out ahead in the stock market, you only had to be right on 60 percent of your decisions. Cliff felt up to the task, but he was never sure how to make that calculation. Did his decision not to buy Kodak count only once? What if he didn't buy it tomorrow and the next day? Would that be three decisions?

Whatever Cliff made of the 60 percent rule, he also knew that you couldn't make money without taking some sort of action. He remembered an old quote from Dash Quillen, one of the few senior people at Rutherford & Hayes who gave him the time of day. It went something like this: "When there is danger in standing still, and danger in moving ahead, one should take the path that is incident to the latter course." The quotation wasn't original with Dash. He attributed it to a guy named Castlereagh, who apparently represented Great Britain at something called the Congress of Vienna. Lord Castlereagh, it was. The name had a nice ring to it, and so did the quotation.

Cliff looked back at his Kodak file. Should he short the damn stock instead of just leaving it alone? That didn't seem so clear either. When Cliff went short, he vastly preferred that the company in question be hemorrhaging cash or unable to get Price Waterhouse et al. to sign off on its accounting principles. Kodak was far from fitting the bill. The status quo could go on for years. And the fact that the company wasn't guaranteed twenty-first-century leadership didn't mean it wouldn't end up achieving it. Besides, when you're short, you don't want to be short for long, and you should think extra hard before betting against a blue chip. Shorting is a completely different enterprise than buying, and Cliff didn't get into it unless the odds were avalanched in his favor.

Damn! When Cliff looked at it that way, he realized that, technically speaking, his decision not to buy Kodak had been balanced by his decision not to *short* it. His success ratio was back down to 50 percent, even before the story had played itself out. Not good enough. You didn't have to be Lester Thurow to see that Cliff was stuck in a zero-sum game.

But Cliff didn't really care so much about zero-sum games these days. He still couldn't get over the fact that the great Kyle Hooperman had bought shares of URLybirds. How the mighty had fallen. Trace had asked Cliff to write her a crib-sheet review of why the stock was such a sucker play. This is what he came up with.

1. Earnings were a joke.

The prospectus for the URLybirds' offering indicated that earnings had been $1 per share in 1998. The whisper number at the offering was $3 per share for 1999. Earnings were tripling. Wowie, zowie. Trust me, Trace, it's a farce. Does the mother of triplets really expect to hatch nine of them the next time around? More likely, there won't *be* a next time around, which was precisely what happened to URLybirds. They had generated $3 per share by selling the rights to olympicgames.com and a few other names in their portfolio, and they only did that to goose the numbers prior to the public offering. Everyone at the luncheon seemed excited that they had finally found a profitable Internet play. People were comparing URLybirds to Network Solutions, just because they were both in the domain-name business. But Network Solutions was in the business of *registering* domain names, not selling their own supply. They just got a buyout offer from Verisign for something like $20 billion. URLybirds' earnings were nothing but a one-time gain.

2. Names dry up.

Did investors really think URLybirds could keep their act going forever? I'm reminded of Patten Corporation, the land developer that became a hot stock in the mid-'80s by parceling up blocks of New Hampshire and Vermont and selling them to delusional, nouveau riche land barons. The scheme didn't last very long. Will Rogers may have said "Land's the best investment. They ain't making any more of it," but he never said anything about land companies. Patten's day in the sun lasted two years, max.

Even Disney faced a variation of the finiteness problem. In the early '90s animated hits like *The Lion King* and *Aladdin* became an integral part of Disney's growth rate. Investors pushed the stock up even though the quality of earnings was clearly suspect. I mean, you just can't pull off a hit like those every year. *Pocahontas* was no *Lion King*. By 1996, earnings went south and the stock did nothing for about three years.

As for URLybirds, their future was even bleaker. In ten years, all they'd be left with would be the dregs of the domain-name universe—things like chickenliver.com and hoedown.com, which they'd probably end up selling for $1 apiece on eBay.

3. Litigation gives, and litigation takes away.

Check that. In ten years, they might not have anything at all. The company had gotten into serious hot water by going into the people business, buying up names like kimbasinger.com and even newtgingrich.com. Boy, were they desperate! Then they sought large sums from the beleaguered souls whose names they had bought, which was close enough to extortion to get the Feds interested. No more than a few weeks after the IPO, the government finally got around to creating "cybersquatting" laws that had URLybirds written all over them. Their business *was* extortion. And pretty soon after that, there was the matter of the class action suit from poor-sport shareholders who went down with the ship and didn't appreciate the timing of the IPO. The company's legal fees alone were something like 50 cents per share—maybe higher.

The best you could say was that, by now, the stock was way down. Analysts were starting to calculate the company's "carcass value"; URLybirds might be worth more dead than alive. It was even true that if the legal problems were settled, a major expense would be eliminated in one stroke. And maybe a suitor was around the corner, who knew? But carcass value only applied because the stock was 75 percent lower than at the time it went public. You don't go from being a growth stock to a value stock without incredible interim carnage. Kyle Hooperman had been around long enough to know that. And he hadn't gotten to where he was by taking fliers. He was too smart for that.

So what the hell was he doing in this stock? It doesn't add up.

It was now 11:26 P.M., one of Cliff's three favorite times of day or night. His favorite was, of course, 11:11, for its digital simplicity. Next there was 12:36; whether you added the first three digits or multiplied them, you'd get the fourth. The reason 11:26 made the list was more personal. It was Cliff's birthday.

Sometimes he was in bed by 11:26, but Cliff had some extra energy left over from his exhausting day of not buying and not shorting Kodak. He put on his bathrobe and trudged to his study, home of his 486 AST Advantage computer complete with Windows 3.1 and a 28.8 modem. Prior owner: Charlemagne. The damn thing still worked, though, just not at the pace that any of his day-trading brethren would tolerate. And unbeknownst to Cliff, there was a little surprise waiting for him when he opened his e-mail stash.

CHAPTER 4

To: CliffCav@shamus.net
From: DickTracy77@mindspring.com
Re: Unusual Suspect

Cliff, here's what I've got so far. I think you should find it useful.—Trace

Today I talked to Lila Fitzpatrick, one of the victims of URLybirds. I asked her all sorts of questions about the company and her experience with it. Clearly she didn't know the first thing about their business, so I'm figuring it must have been Hooperman's call all the way. But even though she lost $25,000, somehow I think she felt it was worth the gamble and that they were just unlucky it didn't work out.

As Lila and I got to talking, I discovered something you might find of interest: She was infuriated with Hooperman because of an entirely different move he had made. The episode dated back to before Hooperman took over her account. She said she had bought 1,000 shares of Pepsi-Cola at $5 per share and placed it as one of her core holdings. Her hope was to one day live off the dividends, and she thought she had made it clear to Hooperman when he assumed her account that she didn't want to touch the shares themselves. But he sold 500 shares at around the same time he was bailing out of URLybirds, and she was livid about it. I can't say whether she was angry enough to kill him. He had been managing her money without incident for over 15 years. But she added that the very first instruction she gave to her new portfolio manager was that Pepsi was a sacred cow.

Cliff scrolled down in hopes of finding more, but there was nothing to be found. That was it. A dead end.

He laughed at himself for the mess he had created. Trace's prior e-mails had been festooned with minutiae such as the time of the interview, the interviewee's wardrobe, and the way the sun shone down on the participants. Flowery stuff, and none of it necessary. Addendum 2a to Trace's contract said that all he wanted were facts with which he could come to some sort of conclusion. And this is what he got. *Double sigh.*

Given that he was online already, it was a simple matter to check that PepsiCo was trading at around $30 per share—about where Cliff expected. But when he downloaded a long-term chart onto the screen, he noticed something peculiar. According to the chart, the only time the stock was at $5 per share was in and around the 1987 crash—at which point Hooperman was already managing Lila Fitzpatrick's money. So why did Trace say that Lila had bought it herself, before Hooperman came on the scene?

This curiosity of timing didn't have the impact of, say, the Zapruder film, but it sent Cliff into a quandary. He knew that for all of Trace's misguided prose, whether overly flowerly or overly compact, she was a stickler for accuracy. It was no coincidence that her error account had never been tapped. So why did she go to the trouble of mentioning this $5 nonsense when all she could accomplish was to contradict herself? There could be only one answer, and Cliff wasn't sure he liked it.

The basic problem was that PepsiCo wasn't really trading for $5 per share in 1987 or any other time on the chart, never mind first appearances. The actual price of the stock at that moment in 1987 was $5 × 2 × 3, or $30 per share. Why? Because if you looked closely, you'd see that the stock had split 3-for-1 in 1990 and 2-for-1 in 1996.

Ah, stock splits. The most indispensable market wrinkles you could ever find. Not to mention the most annoying and the most overrated.

Indispensable because without them, you might have to pay $100,000 for a single share of IBM, American Express, or practically anything else that's been around for a while. Splits bring prices back to reasonable levels, thereby winning praise from most individual investors.

The annoying part is that if you think in terms of the actual price when you bought—and who doesn't?—there's no way of comparing your purchase price to the current price unless you know how many splits have come in between. Fortunately, brokerage statements come to the rescue by creating "split-adjusted" prices for you. Stock-price charts do much the same thing.

The overrated part refers to the notion that stock splits create instantaneous wealth. It's not so. Yes, stocks often do perk up a bit following the declaration of a split, because individual investors truly are more attracted to lower share prices. But splits are often announced in the context of other good news the company might have, so *that* news might be the actual propellant, not the split itself. Perhaps we shouldn't quibble over the source of our good fortune, but it's worth reminding ourselves that 100 shares at $60 apiece aren't worth any more than the old 50 shares at $120 apiece.

Back to the task at hand. Was Lila being literal when she said that she had bought at $5 per share? Apparently so. But when in the world might PepsiCo have actually traded for just $5?

Cliff thought he had the answer: 1974. That's when just about any big-name stock you could mention—the so-called "Nifty-Fifty"—collapsed after doing nothing but go up for a decade. Little things spooked the market back then. Ridiculously high valuations, the oil crisis, a President's resignation; stuff like that. And as Cliff got the extra-long stock-price chart on his screen, he could see that PepsiCo got as low as a mere 18 cents per share that year.

Split-adjusted, of course. Since 1974, the stock had had three 3-for-1 splits and one 2-for-1 split, so the actual trading price at that time was $3 \times 3 \times 3 \times 2$, or 54 times the price on the chart. Alas, 54 times 18 cents was in the neighborhood of $10 per share. Too high.

At that moment, Cliff noticed something he hadn't picked up on before. According to Trace, Lila said she had bought shares in "Pepsi-Cola," not PepsiCo. When in the goddamn world had it changed its name?

Cliff glanced at the clock. It was 11:30 P.M., not the ideal time to reach Pepsi's investor relations department. Fortunately, he knew a trader in Merrill Lynch's Hong Kong office who was smart, equipped with immense databases, and, best of all, awake.

"Deng, it's Cliff Cavanaugh. Was just saying my bedtime prayers and I thought of you."

"Yeah, right," Deng said. "What's the matter? Can't you get the Nikkei opening online?"

"Um, yeah, I can," Cliff said. "Looks like it's up 150 points, as a matter of fact. But I've got a different sort of question for you."

Deng was surprisingly easy on Cliff, considering that no one with any sort of life calls halfway around the world to find out PepsiCo's corporate genealogy and share price information. The name change turned out to be the easy part; Deng readily checked that Pepsi had changed its name from Pepsi-Cola to PepsiCo in 1965. The change was too bad, really. "Pepsi-Cola" was one of the great corporate anagrams of all time, being a rearrangement of "Episcopal." But the share price question was a wee bit tougher.

"You want what?"

"You heard me, Deng. I want to know if Pepsi-Cola ever traded at $5 per share, real time."

"Easier said than done, I'm afraid," Deng said. "Our electronic files are all split-adjusted. I'm not sure there's any way of getting at unadjusted prices."

"Do you have any of those old SRC chart books?" Cliff asked. Before the Internet came around, Securities Research Corporation had a tidy little business of mailing out clunky stock-price books each month to institutional clients.

"I think we do, as a matter of fact," Deng said. There was an unmistakable pause on the line. "You really expect me to go through all of those things?"

"It's a service business," Cliff said. "Besides, it's not everybody who thinks of you in their bedtime prayers."

Deng said, "Can the prayer angle. I just want a share of whatever you're making on this bet. Just a sec."

Deng returned with a stack of books that even the Library of Congress had sent to a landfill by now. The Internet had rendered most charting services obsolete, except for those occasions when the desired prices were older than the electronic databases. Like now.

"Okay, I'm all set. I keep going until I hit $5 a share, right?"

Cliff said, "You got it."

Cliff figured the whole exercise wouldn't take very long. They had a head start, after all, and each chart book covered 12 years at a pop. All Deng had to do was survey the prices and watch for splits, but Cliff wasn't expecting many splits in those days. The search dragged on, though. Every time Deng had to open up a new book, Cliff's long-distance bill was adding another zero.

"You still there, Deng?"

"Still here."

More silence. The sound of the chart books hitting the floor was becoming more and more like a wrecking ball. But patience is a virtue, and virtue has its rewards.

"Got it!" Deng shouted out.

"No shit?"

"No shit at all, Cliff my man. It's $5 a share I'm looking at, no question about it. Does this win the bet for you?"

"Not exactly, no," Cliff said. "All I need to know is when it happened."

Deng said, "Looks to me like May of 1939."

He'd said *1939*. It was time for another phone call.

■ ■ ■

"Hello," a soft voice murmured.

"Trace, is that you?"

"No, it's Madame Bovary. Of course it's me." Trace lived in a Soho loft with four other aspiring actresses, but the number Cliff used was her personal cell phone.

"Sorry, I forgot that the Lennon Sisters don't share your line." Pause. "Trace, I've made a most unpleasant discovery."

"You had asparagus for dinner?"

"Not quite, and I'm afraid your stand-up act will have to wait," Cliff said. "Can you tell me precisely how Lila Fitzpatrick escaped from her nursing home to shoot Kyle Hooperman?"

"Oops," Trace said.

"Oops is right. I sacrificed the first half of my beauty sleep figuring it out."

Trace said, "Oh, dear. I was just trying to be economical with my reports, like you requested. But I never doubted that you'd get to the bottom of it."

Cliff didn't like the thought of Trace flattering him in an effort to avoid his wrath. The worst part was that it always seemed to work, though this time she might be pushing her luck. If she had actually conducted her Fitzpatrick interview at a nursing home, it might be time for a little talk.

"Trace, just so you know, 85-year-old women aren't our primary suspects here," Cliff said.

"You're right, you're right, a thousand pardons," Trace said. "All I can say is that she didn't sound that old over the phone. But, for future reference, what's the cutoff? I mean, how young does a woman have to be before we start worrying about her?"

"Frankly, I'd be stunned if it was a woman at all."

"You would?"

"Trace, ninety-nine percent of crimes like this one are committed by men. You didn't know that?"

"I guess I never thought about it. I figured everyone was fair game."

Trace felt weirdly offended. Would she actually prefer that the murderer was a woman? And what about the gun? The Colt Government Model was a diminutive little thing, in the same category as Nancy Reagan's fabled "itty-bitty gun." Didn't that raise the chances of a woman being the killer? Or maybe that notion was even more sexist. Would a man use a woman's gun to divert suspicion?

It was time to change the subject.

"Anyway, you'd have been proud of me," she said. "I figured out what Lila Fitzpatrick's annual return was on the stock, using your method. Wanna guess what it was?"

Cliff wondered whether anything in the world could be less interesting than guessing Lila Fitzpatrick's stock market returns, but he was too tired to protest. Maybe he was even curious. Had Trace finally gotten the hang of calculating returns? He listened benignly as Trace explained how Lila had multiplied her money by a factor of 108 times 6, or 648. The 108 figure came from all of the splits, and the 6 came from the absolute increase in the share price, from 5 to 30. An initial investment of $5,000 had turned into more than $3 million.

The brokerage handbooks will tell you that the secret of long-term wealth is *compounding*. Even ordinary-looking gains can become significant if you give them enough time. At first glance, a 648-fold gain—or 64700 percent—looked like it might require something astronomical, like 30 percent per year, to achieve. But Trace, apt pupil that she was, knew better.

"Did you know that the 61st root of 648 is 1.112?" she asked.

The calculator on Cliff's computer wasn't into roots. For that, he had to go to DOS and switch into calculator mode. But that required the energy of a younger man, the way he was when this conversation had begun.

"The roots of money are all evil," he said.

But without the 61st root, the calculation was dead in the water. The significance of the root was that, each year, on average, for 61 years, the Pepsi investment had multiplied in value by a factor of 1.112, equivalent to just an 11.2 percent annual increase. Even Bob Barker would have guessed that a higher figure was required. And the 11.2 percent figure didn't even count Lila's dividend income. For the year at hand, Pepsi was paying out 52 cents per share, giving Lila Fitzpatrick just over $56,000 per year, pretax, all because of a $5,000 investment she made in 1939.

As Cliff regretted ever explaining this procedure in the first place, he realized that all of the brokerage handbooks had been pulling the wool over his eyes. All his life, he had rightly believed that even a modest-looking annual return could lead to a lot of money if you gave it enough time. That's what long-term investing was all about. And that's what Trace's arithmetic seemed to show for the now fabulously wealthy Lila Fitzpatrick.

But 61 years? So what if an 11.2 percent return gives you a 648-fold gain in 61 years? By that time, you're too old to enjoy it! Here Lila is, fussing over a sale of a stupid 500 shares, not out of 1,000, but out of—what was it?—1,000 times three times three times three times two times two: 108,000 stinking goddamn shares! The more Cliff thought about it, even Lila's capital gains tax gripe wasn't entirely well-founded. Surely, Hooperman's strategy was to peel off a bit of PepsiCo at the same time he was taking a loss on URLybirds, thereby creating a "wash" in the eyes of the IRS. Okay, so maybe he could have kept his client better informed. Basic communication seemed to be Hooperman's blind spot. But the old bat didn't have all that much to worry about.

Cliff said, "Trace, words can't possibly express how proud I am of you. But pretty soon the lullaby you hear is going to sound a lot like my snoring. We're still on for tomorrow morning at Rutherford & Hayes's office, though, aren't we? Ten o'clock sharp?"

Trace said, "Wouldn't miss it for the world."

CHAPTER 5

If Rutherford & Hayes was ever truly reeling from the loss of Kyle Hooperman, it didn't take long for the memory to fade. The day the news broke had been full of gasps, coffee-machine huddles, and film crews from WNBC, WNET, WOR, and a few other Ws. But a week later, the only thing amiss was the eerie emptiness of Hooperman's plush twenty-first-floor office, a vacancy that a dozen or so lesser managers had already kindly offered to fill. Sometime in between, a prankster had taken apart the handset on Hooperman's phone and inserted some thinly sliced smoked salmon, just to make sure that the new occupant's first purchase order was a memorable one. Mourning, Wall Street style.

Trace wasn't the sort who made effusive apologies, but she made damn sure she was at R&H's main reception desk at 10:00 sharp. As she arrived, she noticed a man in a blue pin-striped suit sitting on one of the couches in the waiting area. He was thumbing through that morning's *Wall Street Journal* and seemed preoccupied. He had medium-length brown hair that was thinning but hadn't yet made him into a peninsula head. His face was wiry and more familiar than she was expecting. For Trace, this was foreign territory.

It was Cliff Cavanaugh.

"Omigod," Trace said. "I didn't recognize you. You look. . . ." She just kept shaking her head. Cliff was pretty sure she meant to say "fabulous."

"Just because I quit my day job doesn't mean I pitched my day clothes," he said. "You want to compose yourself before you meet a few more suits?"

"No, I'm okay. Carry on."

At Cliff's insistence, their first stop was the trading floor. Like many of the large brokerage firms, Rutherford & Hayes had its own trading area, which was like a scale model of the floor of the New York Stock Exchange, except that participants wore white shirts instead of those snappy NYSE traders' jackets. If this particular day was business as usual, business was good indeed. It was just a few minutes past 10:00, and already 100 million shares had changed hands on the Big Board. One broker shouted triumphantly upon seeing a block trade of 50,000 shares of Du Pont appear on the ticker overhead. Like a concert violinist or a master glass blower, he took pride in his work.

Cliff was taking more than passing interest in the ticker. Finally, he made a clicking sound from the side of his mouth, as if he was handling a Bichon Frise at Westminster.

"Oh well," he said.

"What's the matter?"

"Nothing, I'm just out a little money, that's all," Cliff said. "I bet that Kodak would open lower today, and it's up a point and three-quarters."

"I thought you didn't get into that sort of thing," Trace said. "Or did you suddenly change your mind?"

"Nah, it was just a private bet with my friend Deng in Hong Kong. He probably had some aftermarket information and was just taking me for a ride, but that's okay. I owed him one. I'm pretty sure it's a business expense, not a gambling debt. I can write it off."

As Cliff's gaze returned to ground level, he saw an older man wearing a red-and-white striped shirt topped off with a navy-blue bow tie, and that could mean only one thing.

"Dash!" Cliff shouted.

The man looked over, and a broad grin slowly appeared. "If it isn't Cliff Cavanaugh, my favorite dropout in the whole wide world. I thought you might be stopping by."

Cliff walked up and shook the man's hand vigorously, then clasped his left hand around the handshake for good measure. Trace could tell that Cliff wanted to give the guy a great big hug, but the trading floor decorum won out.

"Trace, I'd like you to meet none other than Dash Quillen."

"Enchanté," Dash said, offering his oversized hand Trace's way and genuflecting ever so slightly. He was seventy-five if he was a day, but he was as smooth as ever. He still had a bushy head of white hair; the only bald spot was in back, and you had to be over six-foot-two to catch a glimpse of it. His oversized eyebrows were like a pair of fluffy cumulus clouds that had maybe a hint of rain. He seemed slightly tanned, even in February—yet more proof that life was treating him well.

"Dash heads the fixed-income trading operation," Cliff said.

Dash quickly amended that. "In a past life, anyway," he said. "Nowadays, I come in twice a week, mainly just to help train the new recruits. Keeps me out of trouble."

"Director of fixed-income trading emeritus, then," Cliff gushed. "Dash was my mentor. Taught me absolutely everything I know about people and money."

"Well, someone had to, Cliff my man," Dash said. "Hope it's paying off in this second life of yours."

"Natch," Cliff said. "But not in this case—at least not yet. Naturally, I'll feel a whole lot better once you tell us who inside the firm might have benefited from Hooperman's death."

Dash smiled a big bright-white smile that made you forget he predated fluoride. "Hey, I thought that's why we hired you. To dig up that sort of dirt."

"What can I tell you?" Cliff parried. "I'm just a career ingrate, that's all."

Dash said, "Truthfully, all I know is that Hooperman's accounts were split between Dave Lenci and Ginny Truesdale. Dave you probably know already. Ginny came over from PaineWebber a couple of years ago."

"So how was it that those two inherited the accounts?" Trace asked.

Dash and Cliff looked at one another and, practically in unison, said, "Cummings."

Dash leaned Trace's way. "It's our director of operations, Sean Cummings. He's not exactly Cliff's favorite person around here."

"Not so," Cliff said. "Cummings is the most likable bean-counting neo-Nazi I ever met. He's still calling the shots?"

Dash said, "Sure is, at least on all the nasty stuff. You know: staffing, allotments, reviews, things like that. But there are still a few little fiefdoms he doesn't control." Dash started to chuckle. "You should have seen his face when he found out that you were the private investigator we hired."

Cliff proceeded to tell Dash about URLybirds and his list of disgruntled or potentially disgruntled clients. Dash listened patiently but finally shook his head. "Cliff, I know what you're saying, but clients don't always react the way you think they're going to," he said. "Let me tell you a story.

"Back in the early '80s, we managed the account of a lady named Beatrice Honeycutt, may God rest her soul. Her account was loaded with fixed-income securities—corporates, Ginnie Maes, Treasuries, you name it. Well, the bond market was soaring, and sometime in 1984 she came in for a meeting with her portfolio manager—you remember Bob Hoogstratten?"

"Sure do," Cliff said. "Couldn't forget old Bondo Bob."

"Anyway, Hoogstratten was feeling pretty good. Here he was presiding over one of the great bond rallies of all time, and old lady Honeycutt was making money hand over fist. He's got her almost exclusively in longer maturities, which is exactly where you want to be when interest rates are coming down. So he figured she was going to tell him what a miracle worker he was; but when she gets in, she starts screaming at him. She points to some Treasury bond in her portfolio and shrieks, 'This bond is only yielding 8 percent. Two years ago, it was yielding 14 percent!' Well, Hoogstratten tried telling her that the only reason for the decline in yield was that the price of the bond itself had gone way up, but she didn't understand. All she saw was a lower yield, even though her portfolio had grown substantially and her income stream was identical."

Cliff burst out laughing. "Good thing she died before the long bond hit 5 percent," he said.

Dash said, "The point is, you never know what's going to piss clients off."

"Hear! Hear!" Cliff said.

"So what happened to Bondo Bob?" Trace asked.

"Things got worse in a hurry," Dash recalled. "A few years later, he was part of a team that was trying to drum up some institutional business. They were giving a presentation to the State of Georgia pension fund, or something like that. Apparently, all was going well until one of the committee members asked if Rutherford & Hayes did duration analysis."

"Of course we do duration analysis," Cliff said.

"Sure, you and I know that," Dash said. "But this committee member probably just wanted to show he knew what duration *was*, that's all.

"Well, what is it?" Trace asked.

"You want the Algebra I version or the calculus version?" Cliff asked.

"Algebra I, smarty-pants," Trace said. "But I'd prefer connect-the-dots."

"Here goes," Cliff said. "The duration of a bond is a weighted average. The time until each payment period is weighted by the amount of the payment, including the principal payback at maturity.

So if the bond happens to be a zero-coupon bond, then duration equals the time until maturity. If it's your normal bond with a semi-annual coupon payment, its duration is way less than its maturity — maybe 10 years instead of 30. The higher the coupon, the shorter the duration, because you're essentially getting your money sooner."*

"Thanks for keeping it simple," Trace said.

"Anyway," Dash continued, "Hoogstratten could have answered the question with a simple yes or no, but instead he says something like, 'Yes, we've got a gal in our New York office who handles that.' At which point, one of the women on the committee sat back in her seat and inquired in one of those slow, syrupy, Southern voices, 'And does this *gal* have a name?'

"They might as well have ended the meeting right then and there," Dash continued. "It wasn't too long afterward that Cummings gave Hoogstratten the heave-ho."

"No surprise there," Cliff said. "With Cummings, clients come first and employees come two-hundredth."

"And he's at it again," Dash said.

"What do you mean?" Cliff asked.

"You don't know?"

"I don't know anything."

"Hughie Szabo was fired," Dash said.

"Who the hell is Hughie Szabo?" Cliff asked.

"Yeah, I guess you wouldn't know him," Dash said. "He was only here nine months or so. He was a muni trader. Handled local bonds — you know, like Triborough Bridge & Tunnel, MTA bonds,

---

* If Trace had insisted on the calculus version, Cliff was prepared to say that duration equals the negative of the derivative of the price-yield function, so a bond's duration tells you how much the price of the bond will change in response to changes in interest rates, which is one of the cornerstones of bond management. But he didn't want to interrupt Dash's story.

stuff like that. Apparently, some clients bitched about the prices they got, and the big boys looked into his record. Out he went."

"But our problem is different," Trace said. "Just yesterday, I came across a client who didn't even blink after Hooperman cost her a few dozen grand with URLybirds."

When Cliff had first mentioned URLybirds, he thought Dash might have ruptured his spleen. This time it was down to just a plain wince. "Not exactly a Rutherford & Hayes success story," Dash said. "If that's why Hooperman was killed, we'll probably have a few more corpses around here before long."

Neither Trace nor Cliff could tell whether he was joking.

CHAPTER 6

Sean Cummings was one of those guys who goes bald early and then looks the same for 25 years. His career was no different. If you bypass his years as an archery counselor at summer camp, Rutherford & Hayes was the only employer on his resume.

He started as a portfolio assistant in the days when every single purchase or sale meant filling out multicolored forms in quadruplicate. The higher-ups were impressed by his attention to detail. They made him superintendent of supplies, which basically involved making sure everyone had enough fluorescent bulbs and Post-it notes to properly do their jobs. But Cummings had come a long way. As the firm's director of operations, he was now perched in a corner office on the twenty-second floor. He had been a partner of R&H for over a decade.

Behind his back, Cummings was dubbed "Fluffer," but not because there was anything soft or cuddly about him. People at R&H just figured that his fascination with minutiae must be tied to fluffing up the firm for potential sale. But Cliff wasn't buying into that theory one bit. True, if R&H ever got bought out, Cummings could go parasailing for the rest of his life. But for someone who danced only to the tune of corporate intrigue, it would be the worst thing that ever happened. After all, his job let him play *Stratego* every day, with human pieces.

"Well, well. Cliff Cavanaugh. The famous shamus himself. May I ask what brings you here?"

"Just stopping by," Cliff said, poking his head into the doorway. One of Cummings's office design innovations was to replace every inside opaque wall with glass, so no one could sneak up on anyone else.

"Funny how you never stopped by until Hooperman was killed," Cummings said.

"Ya got me there, Sean," Cliff said. Cummings didn't like being called by his first name, which didn't sound tough enough for his tastes. It was better than Fluffer, though.

"May I introduce my colleague, Tracy de Grandpre?"

Cummings walked toward them. His signature giant steps didn't quite fit his 28-inch inseam. He looked almost bowlegged. He put on a big smile and stretched out his right hand. "Sean Cummings. Pleased to make your acquaintance."

"I've heard a lot about you," Trace said.

Cummings shifted his eyes toward Cliff for just an instant, then beckoned them both inside. Space was not a problem; that much was certain. Cummings's desk was in the far corner, and behind his chair was a 220-degree view of lower Manhattan and Staten Island. You couldn't do better without being in the cockpit of a DC-9. Between the doorway and his desk there was a sitting area with four black leather chairs, a red-and-blue Karastan rug, and a table consisting of an inch-thick rectangular glass slab supported at the ends by two copper replicas of *Vertebrae*, by Henry Moore.

"So, does 'just stopping by' mean that you're going to interrogate me?" Cummings chuckled. "Do I need my lawyer present?"

"You're in the clear so far," Cliff said. "Actually, I have only one simple question for you."

"Shoot," said Cummings, "or can't I use that word during a murder investigation?"

"Heh, heh. You can make any joke you want to," Cliff said, "as long as you tell me how was it that Dave Lenci and Ginny Truesdale happened to get Hooperman's accounts."

The backhanded implication was not lost on Cummings, whose public stance was that any Rutherford & Hayes employee was cleaner than Warren Buffett's credit report. "You sound desperate, Cavanaugh."

"Desperate? Hardly. Six months from now you can call me desperate. For now, I'm just curious."

"Well, I hate to spoil your sense of intrigue," Cummings said, "but the reason Lenci and Truesdale won out is that they've been the best producers, period. That's all there is to it."

By "producers," Cummings meant that Lenci and Truesdale had consistently raked in the most commissions, which in turn gave them first dibs on the hottest new issues, not to mention the accounts of a murdered colleague. It was one of many ways that the rich-get-richer game played out within the brokerage world.

"You folks still operating on straight commission?" Cliff asked.

"Not as much as in the old days, no. Probably 75 percent of our managers now take a percentage of the assets under management, as opposed to commissions. That's probably the biggest recent change in the way we do business. Either way, though, those two have been our best managers and clearly deserved Hooperman's accounts."

"I never said otherwise," Cliff said. "I'm just getting information, not accusing anybody. I wouldn't even know Ginny Truesdale if I ran into her."

"Truesdale? She's British, somewhat older than you or I. A bit on the stocky side. Graying at the temples. A little rigid, proper—you know, British, like I said."

Trace commented that the description sounded a lot like a woman she had seen just a few minutes before, on the trading floor. Cliff thought it sounded more like Stonehenge.

"And I hate to be blunt, Cavanaugh, but I doubt either of those two would have killed Hooperman just to get at a few of his accounts."

Cliff knew a lie when he heard one. Not that Lenci or Truesdale necessarily had anything to do with the case, but Cummings sure as hell didn't hate to be blunt.

Cliff said, "It just so happens I have a pet theory on that."

"Which you're dying for me to ask about?"

"You got it," Cliff said. "When someone is killed, we look for motive, right?"

Cummings nodded.

"The only problem is that the people looking for motives are non-murderers. I mean, we could look at every facet of a victim's interpersonal relationships and conclude that nothing would be enough to kill him for, but we had better acknowledge that *we* wouldn't kill anyone over *anything*, right? It doesn't change the fact that the victim is dead. Someone killed him. That much is for sure, and they did so whether we like the reasons or not. So, until we find the murder weapon stashed in someone's desk drawer, our suspect list had better include anyone and everyone who either was pissed at Hooperman while he was alive or is better off now that he's gone."

"Fair enough, Cavanaugh," Cummings responded. "But I warn you. Any false accusations against one of our portfolio managers, or anyone on our staff, and I'll send your retainer into permanent escrow, you understand?"

"Does that include Hughie Szabo?"

"How do you know about Szabo?"

"Dash Quillen just told me. Anything more to the story I should know?"

"Just that he's been replaced by someone who actually knows what he's doing."

"That didn't take long," Cliff said.

"It never does," Cummings said. "People around here understand that if they don't want to deliver, someone else will take their paper route."

Cliff had to hand it to Cummings. Here was a guy in search of his first moral fiber, but he could appear politically correct just by looking out for the bottom line at Rutherford & Hayes. Before he came along, you had a better chance of finding a black person at a Neil Diamond concert than on the R&H trading floor, but Cummings could see that the old-boy, plain vanilla network was bad for business, so he changed it. As for Bondo Bob Hoogstratten, he could have been chasing, ogling, or otherwise harassing his secretary, and Cummings wouldn't have cared. But when a slip of the tongue cost R&H an institutional account, Bondo was outta there, and Cummings ended up looking future-oriented and downright sanctimonious in the process. Not to mention powerful.

"I understand," Cliff said.

■ ■ ■

"What an operator," Trace said as she and Cliff boarded the down elevator. She idly wondered whether Jason Alexander would be interested in title billing for *The Sean Cummings Story*, if indeed there was a place for such a story. Fifteen minutes of chit-chat was about as much as she, the audience, could handle.

"Cummings is a player, that's for sure," Cliff said.

"Did you notice the way he funched his nose?"

"What do you mean?"

"Like this," Trace said. She tightened the muscles above her upper lip. The downward pressure caused two whitish spots to appear in the middle, bony part of her nose. At the same time, her lip protruded in a way that for one horrifying second made the incomparable Tracy de Grandpre into a direct descendant of Cro-Magnon man.

For a moment, Cliff considered covering up the surveillance camera with his suit jacket. The footage would be blackmail material if and when Trace hit the big time. No sense tempting Nicky the Pinkerton's guy and starting him on a life of crime. But the elevator stopped to pick up a few more working stiffs. Trace and Cliff huddled in the corner.

Cliff asked softly, "Cummings did that?"

"He sure did," Trace said, matching Cliff's tone.

"I didn't even notice," Cliff said. "I was probably in the middle of my 'stop at nothing' spiel. I thought I was in pretty good form, didn't you?"

"Yeah, you were in good form all right, but that's not when he did it," Trace said.

"When was it, then?" Cliff asked.

"At no time in particular," Trace said.

"No time in particular?! No, Trace, I'm afraid that's impossible. We're talking about one of the great passive–aggressive creatures of our time. Everything is a calculation with him. Nothing happens by accident. Not ever."

Trace seemed perplexed. "But he talked to us for no particular reason, didn't he?" she asked.

"Hardly," Cliff said. "One look at me and his ego meter took over. In his mind, I was dying at all the evidence of his success, and he wanted to lap it up."

"And were you?"

"Never mind me. When did he funch his damn nose?"

"I'm telling you, it was for no reason. The first time—oh, this is really stupid."

"When?"

"It was when I mentioned my silly error account."

"You mentioned your error account and Cummings funched his nose?"

"That's right."

Cliff began glowing like the Chernobyl reservoir. "Trace, you're a genius."

"I am?"

The elevator had reached the lobby, an open expanse of shiny, orange-toned marble. They pushed their way through the crowd and took the conversation to a spot right next to the R&H-dominated office directory. Cliff was still smiling.

"You sure are. Where did you think the term 'error account' came from?"

"I didn't know it came from anywhere."

"Well, it does, and I can give you an example." Cliff said. "Suppose a client calls up to buy a hot new IPO, but then the stock tanks right after the offering. Tough noogies, right?"

"I guess so," Trace said. "What else could it be?"

"That's the sick part. Every broker I know has a story about clients squawking that they never intended to buy the stock in the first place. Even when they're totally bullshitting, the complaint can end up on Cummings's lap. And he finds it a whole lot easier to charge the broker's error account than to question the client's integrity. It can cost the broker tens of thousands of dollars."

"Did it ever happen to you?"

"Just before I left R&H in 1995, a client called to buy Sysco, the food-service company. I misunderstood and bought Cisco Systems instead. The client apparently didn't read the confirmation we sent, so he didn't realize the mistake until after I left. There was never a problem, basically because my Cisco went up more than his, but the truth was that the error account mechanism gave him a free shot at the best Cisco in town. Ever since then, R&H has gone by ticker symbol, not just name, 'cause it's a lot harder to confuse SYY with CSCO."

"Gotcha," Trace said. "But I was referring to my own error account, not a broker's."

"True, but Cummings didn't know that."

"Are you suggesting that he thought I was mentioning an error account just to try and get a rise out of him? Is he that paranoid?"

Cliff looked at her scornfully.

"I retract the question, your honor."

"You got it," Cliff said. "Remember the first rule of dealing with the terminally passive–aggressive. They will *never* assume that something you say is an accident, because *they* would never say anything by accident. Cummings figured you already knew something about somebody's error account, because why else would you have mentioned it?"

"But what about the other time? All I said was that I recognized Ginny Truesdale from earlier in the morning. What possible reason could Cummings have had for funching his nose?"

"Beats the hell out of me. But, like I said, it wasn't for no reason at all."

CHAPTER 7

If you're looking for a true artist, Edgar Piello is your man. No question about that. Perfection is his goal, and he never stops until he reaches it. He'd have made a terrible investor. Nothing would ever be good enough to buy. He'd do fine when the market was down, and stupendously when it crashed, but the rest of the time he'd be left behind like a finicky shopper on *Supermarket Sweep*. At least Edgar had the good sense to know himself and concentrate on what he did best. He was even able to make concessions now and then, as when he had a client who was in a hurry.

He beamed as he put the finishing touches on his masterpiece. "*Voila!*" he said. "No one will recognize you now."

Trace looked into the mirror and had to agree. Her blond wig was straight out of Mamie van Doren in *High School Confidential*. Her eyeshadow was the turquoise blue of a Bermuda high tide. She had fake eyelashes that stood up like a series of giant quotation marks. Most important of all, there were no freckles. Not one. Edgar's House of Pancake Make-Up had seen to that.

Dave Lenci wasn't going to know what hit him.

■ ■ ■

"A pleasure to meet you, Miss Steinbach."

"Oh, please call me Sandy," Trace said. "And it's nice to meet you, too, Mr. Lenci. Sorry if I'm a bit late."

"No problem whatsoever, Sandy. Have a seat. Can I get you a cup of coffee? Tea? Perrier?"

Trace remembered what Cliff had said about R&H putting its clients first, and it appeared he wasn't kidding. Moral: If you have $3 million in the bank and are contemplating hiring a professional money manager, people will still fawn over you even if you're ten minutes late. Check that. All you need is for someone to *think* you have $3 million in the bank.

She looked around Lenci's office, which was perfectly nice but something of a comedown by Sean Cummings's standards. His desk was more of a standard-issue cherry wood, and it was covered with an assortment of annual reports and manila folders. To the right was a bookcase that offered such titles as *Standard & Poor's Dividend Records, Moody's Credit Reports, Value Line Investment Survey,* and *Nelson's Guide to Institutional Research.* Your basic library from hell. A sign at the end of his desk read "Theodore D. Lenci, Investment Counselor."

Lenci was a tall, dark-haired man with fifty or so years behind him—or, as Rutherford & Hayes's promotional literature might put it, 25 years of investment experience. He was lean as a rail, but any aspirations to healthiness ended there. His face was a sallow oyster gray, as if his capillaries had organized a midlife work stoppage. Too many hours at his desk and too few Tae-Bo tapes. Legend had it that his only exercise consisted of walking to every ATM south of Fulton Street, just to listen to the skiff-skaff of the cash machines.

Now that Kyle Hooperman was gone, Lenci was the most visible and biggest gun in the firm. No one ever accused him of being an investor in Hooperman's class, but he was a legendary salesman, a mirror person *par excellence.* If a client wanted value investing, that was his specialty. If a client wanted hand-holding, he was Joe Compassionate. By now, Lenci had more kindred spirits than the *Psychic*

Friends Network, and all of them were paying customers. He lived on a breathtaking waterfront property in Sands Point, which he shared year-round with his free-spirited wife, their two bratty kids, and countless phone calls from nervous clients. Lenci was thought to be the only person in the world to have been profiled by *Architectural Digest*, *Smart Money*, and *Negligent Father* magazines.

"Tough day in the market today, but I came out all right," he said with a smile. "When my screen is blue, I'm not." He motioned without great subtlety to the Quotron behind him. He had one of those screen displays where up stocks are shown in blue, and down stocks in red. Trace saw all of two red symbols amid thirty or forty blue ones. Not a bad showing, particularly on the dreary day at hand. It's now a bit past 4:00 P.M., and the Dow had closed with a loss of over 200 points.

"The Federal Reserve made noises about raising rates again, so financial stocks were hit pretty hard," he continued. "We had already moved out of financials a few weeks ago, so we weren't affected that much. That's what we try to do here at Rutherford & Hayes. We try to stay one step ahead of the crowd."

"Well," Trace said, "as I said on the phone, what I'm really looking to do is to grow my money for the long term. I'm willing to take some risks, and I don't mind riding out a few bumpy patches along the way."

"I agree with your philosophy 100 percent," said Lenci. "I'm sure that's what your uncle would have wanted."

"My uncle? Oh, of course, yes. He was a good old-fashioned long-term investor," Trace said. She had momentarily forgotten that her sudden wealth was supposed to have come at the expense of her Uncle Harold, who had died tragically in a Tierra del Fuego ballooning accident.

"But I also have a few questions I was hoping you could answer. I hope they're not stupid questions," Trace said.

"There's no such thing as a stupid question from a client," Lenci said.

"Well, you haven't heard mine yet," Trace said. She reached into her pocketbook and pulled out a small lavender memo pad. The notes that she and Cliff had worked on were copied there, in her handwriting. "Okay, here's one. When you buy a stock, where does the money go?"

"The money? Where does it go?"

"That's right. Where does it go?"

"Well, um, it goes to the person you bought the stock from," Lenci said. "That's the purpose of the stock exchange. It brings buyers and sellers together."

"What about if the company is issuing shares for the first time?" Trace asked. "Then I'm not buying it from anybody else, am I?"

"No, you're not. In that case, your money goes directly to the company. Are you interested in participating in IPOs?"

"IPOs?" Trace echoed.

"Initial public offerings," Lenci explained.

Trace got a kick out of Lenci's stoic expression. Being in disguise with $3 million to spend was a great way to spend the afternoon. For $20 million, she could probably ask him who won the Civil War and still get an earnest reply.

"Oh, yes, I'm definitely interested in IPOs," Trace said.

"You don't mind the risks?"

"Not at all. Here's how I figure it. When a company comes to market, it is given a value, right? Something like $10 a share for 15 million shares?"

"Something like that, yes."

"So that means the market says the company is worth $150 million, right?"

"Can't disagree with you there."

"But that's before the company ever gets the money. To me, that means that the stock can't help but go up when the offering is completed, because then it has $150 million in the bank that it never had before."

Lenci was aware that Trace's arithmetic wasn't quite right. For starters, the underwriters of the offering would typically receive a commission on the order of seven percent. And sometimes the company's officers would be selling a portion of their shares, in which case they would pocket some money that was otherwise destined for the company. What Trace was really talking about was the difference between a "pre-money" and "post-money" valuation, which the market tries to allow for. Nonetheless, her point wasn't entirely off-base. A public offering is a source of momentum as well as cash, and if that cash is properly deployed, so much the better.

"Very perceptive of you. But I have to warn you that it doesn't always work out just like that," Lenci said.

"But haven't there been a ton of new offerings that went through the roof?" Trace asked. "I've heard stories of people tripling their money overnight, just because they got in early. Are you telling me I can't do that?"

"No, but I would caution you that there will be an occasional disappointment as well."

"Like URLybirds?"

"Yes, like URLybirds. That would be a great example of one that didn't work out."

Trace was waiting for a flinch, but she never got it. Either he never bought any shares or he was bucking for a Tony Award.

Lenci continued, "But you also have to understand that even for the best new issues, only a limited number of investors get to be there at the very beginning. Most new shares are sold to institutions and friends of the company. There's not much left for retail clients."

"Who cares about retail clients?" Trace asked.

"Well," Lenci started to say. He looked down at this desk, as if it could complete his thought for him. "You see, you're a retail client. An individual investor."

"I am?" Trace asked. "Oh dear, I didn't know that. I guess I've been called worse, though."

Lenci laughed. "I can see you'll be a good sport. Now don't get me wrong, yours is a good-sized account. But we have plenty of bigger accounts who can't understand why they don't get shares of every last offering. Believe me, I'd do it if I could, but I can't control the basic laws of supply and demand.

"Are you considering a discretionary account, or would you like to be part of the decision-making process?" he asked.

"Oh, I'd love to be part of the process," Trace answered. She interpreted the slight downtick in Lenci's shoulders to mean that she may have picked his second choice. "Communication is very important to me. If I didn't want communication with my portfolio manager, I'd just buy some mutual funds and leave it at that."

Lenci nodded.

Trace continued, "I'll give you an example. Earlier this month, a friend of mine panicked when a company called 3-D Live caused some sort of ruckus. You know the stock I'm talking about?"

Still no flinch. "Yes, I do. I was on the phone with several clients that night. They were concerned that the company might not be an attractive holding any more. Frankly, I agreed with them."

"You mean you stayed after work just to keep your clients well informed?" Trace asked. Her eyelashes were fluttering like a hungry hummingbird, just to make damn sure he knew she was impressed.

Lenci's body language took a turn for the better. "That's right," he said. "I was phoning clients until nine o'clock."

Lenci was actually in something of a trap. He couldn't claim to be attentive without also admitting that his clients had lost money. He didn't necessarily believe that Sandy Steinbach had set that type of trap for him, but she had already surpassed his expectations. For her part, Trace wondered when Lenci found the time to get new investment ideas if he was always playing a caretaker role. With as many clients as he had, there was probably a stock blowing up in his face on every trading day.

"Naturally, only a few clients were affected," he added.

"Naturally," Trace said.

■ ■ ■

"So what did Linda Greer have to say for herself?" Trace asked.

"She said that Cummings had been cracking down on the firm's trading procedures," Cliff said. "He was adamant that no portfolio managers make their own trades."

"I thought that's what portfolio managers did."

"No, what I mean is that they're supposed to go through the firm's traders rather than calling some over-the-counter dealer and buying something themselves."

"Why?"

"Because if managers are making their own trades, they can, in theory, hide them. Cummings didn't want Rutherford & Hayes to go the way of Barings Bank, so he instituted a policy that created a trail for the entire process."

"So what you're saying is that maybe Ginny Truesdale didn't belong on the trading floor in the first place."

"That's how it looks, all right."

"Geez. No wonder Cummings funched his nose."

"Yep," Cliff said. "But first things first. How'd it go with you and Lenci?"

"Not too bad," Trace said. "I left a touch of the glittery blue eyeshadow on. It doesn't go with my real eyes, though."

"You can wear it as long as you want," Cliff said. "Just make sure it's gone by the time you show up at Ginny Truesdale's door."

"Don't worry about that," Trace said. "But frankly, Lenci put on such a good show that it would be hard to justify looking elsewhere. If I really had the money, I mean. Cliff, I tried not to seem too impressed, but the guy did have something like 38 up stocks and 2 down stocks today. I wonder what his screen looks like on a good day!"

Cliff laughed out loud. "Probably the same," he said.

"What do you mean?"

"Sounds like the old Bobby Vinton ploy to me." Cliff said. "Blue on blue."

Trace didn't realize that she was supposed to say "heartache on heartache." Cliff let it pass.

"I don't know what you're talking about," Trace said. "But I sure as hell don't like the expression on your face."

"Trace, we're on the phone."

"I don't care. I can just see your little smirk from here. And I don't like the word 'ploy' either. Are you telling me I was snookered?"

"No, Sandy Steinbach was snookered."

"Right. How silly of me. I must be a better actress than I thought."

"Here's how it works," Cliff said. "Lenci saw that the market was tanking, which could have affected the entire tone of your meeting. Unacceptable, right? Well, he knew you were coming at 4:00, so, starting at about 3:30, he searched for companies whose stocks were up. Even on a bad day like today, there were 1,100 advances and 1,800 declines, so he had plenty of blue stocks to choose from. He slapped a few on his screen whether he'd heard of them or not, and, in the process, made himself look like a stockpicking genius."

Trace marveled at the investment community's obsession with warding off the inevitable. The whole charade made sense for Lenci in pretty much the same way that the earnings bluff had made sense for the entourage at URLybirds, only more so. By the time one of

Lenci's clients figures out that he isn't a stockpicking genius after all, he has collected three years' worth of management fees.

"So did he tell you what he was doing the night 3-D Live tanked?" Cliff asked.

"He sure did, and it's just as you suspected. According to Lenci, he was phoning clients until nine o'clock or so."

"Did it register with him that you were talking about the night Hooperman was killed?"

"Nope, I don't think he had a clue."

CHAPTER 8

To: CliffCav@shamus.net
From: DickTracy77@mindspring.com
Re: A Couple More Suspects

Cliff, three down, one to go. Here's some background on two other victims of URLybirds.—T

The first person I spoke to was a gentleman named Milton Koenig. He lives on the Upper West Side—not far from you, actually—but I didn't get around to meeting with him up there because he was willing to share some information over the phone. I can't say I know much about him even now. He sounds like he's in his late fifties, maybe sixty. He's a professional musician, and he's been with the New York Philharmonic for basically forever. Plays the contrabassoon, of all things.

Koenig described himself as nothing more than an amateur investor, but frankly he wasn't very convincing. As we talked, I could hear a voice in the background dispensing all sorts of stock tips. At first I thought it was the television, but he told me it was one of those Books on Tape deals. It was a recording of a book called *This Is Not Your Father's Stockpicking Book,* which he said came out sometime in 1995. The chapter he was listening to was on how to pick stocks based on the weather, or something oddball like that. Anyway, I could tell that he was more interested in the tape than in what I had to say. I didn't feel I could tell him to turn the damn thing off, so I kept our conversation brief.

I said I was representing a group of shareholders in a class action suit against URLybirds. He said he lost on the order of

$40,000 on URLybirds. He also said that he hadn't even heard of the company when it came public, but his account with Rutherford & Hayes was a discretionary account, so Hooperman felt free to do what he wanted. But Koenig wasn't interested in joining the suit. He said he had already been down that road before, and it wasn't worth the trouble. "Hmmm," I said to myself. I didn't pursue my thoughts with him, but I'll have more before this e-mail is through.

The other URLybirds investor I spoke with was a woman named Shari Beck, who is an executive with a shipping company or something like that. She keeps a pretty tight schedule and her secretary guards her like the *Mona Lisa,* but I was able to get a few words in late yesterday afternoon. Shari wasn't much interested in the idea of a lawsuit, either. It turns out that she lost $15,000 with URLybirds, but she was quick to point out that she had done extremely well with a host of other IPOs in and around the same time, including Priceline and TheStreet.com. She confirmed that her 25-year-old son Eric had a separate but smaller account with Hooperman, and that he participated in pretty much the same stocks that she did. I haven't spoken to Eric yet, but I intend to. (Oops. Make that three down, two to go.) I'll have to use a different approach with him, though. She all but guaranteed me that he wouldn't be interested in joining the suit.

The noteworthy thing about these two clients is how much more I found out about them after talking with Linda Greer. First of all, you were right about Linda. She's a walking and talking media leak, so I'm pretty happy we're on the same side. She said that Shari Beck was a pretty big deal in the business world and was on the board of directors of several Fortune 500 companies. And she was also no stranger to IPOs. Most of her wealth came from the first investment decision she ever made: Her first year out of college, she invested $10,000 in the initial offering of a company called Intel, which apparently makes semiconductors.

Okay, just kidding. URLybirds didn't ring a bell with me, but Intel I know.

According to Linda, Shari Beck recruited Hooperman specifically to work on her non-Intel portfolio. She didn't want to sell Intel, but she also didn't like the fact that so much of her net worth was concentrated in that one stock. For the record, her son Eric is an only child (the senior Becks are divorced), so his little nest egg started off without any dilution.

Linda Greer said she had never met Milton Koenig, but, as far as she knew, he hadn't gotten rich by playing the cello. As a matter of fact, he wasn't born into wealth, nor was he a self-made man in the traditional sense. Linda was pretty sure that he had won a major legal settlement of some sort, many years ago. That was the basis of the sizable nest egg that he eventually took to Hooperman.

Linda also said that Koenig was at the center of a major blowup in early 1999. It all started when he bought 1,000 shares of a company called PLX Technology at its initial offering. The price was something like $10 per share. The wrinkle was that Rutherford & Hayes didn't have any record of his request, or of his being allotted shares. The stock quickly went to $25 or so, at which point Koenig sold. (Prematurely, I guess. Linda said that as this whole misadventure was playing out, PLX Technology soared to something like $50 per share.)

That's when things really got sticky. Because Koenig hadn't been allotted any shares in the first place, he was trying to sell shares he didn't own. (I'm sure you'll tell me how this is possible. I was too embarrassed to admit to Linda that I didn't have the foggiest idea of what she was talking about.) Rutherford & Hayes eventually resolved the situation by paying Koenig his "rightful" proceeds of $25,000, which she said came right out of Hooperman's pocket.

Please, whatever screwups I may someday make, if you ever dock my error account for that much money, give me a big raise first.

Your starving artist,

Trace.

To: DickTracy77@mindspring.com
From: CliffCav@shamus.net
Re: A Couple More Suspects

Trace, the situation you described with Milton Koenig is actually more common than most people realize—the setup, anyway, if not the payout. Clients of full-service brokerage firms often maintain separate accounts elsewhere, either with another full-service firm or a discount brokerage of some sort. That's life.

Which is not to say that full-service brokers aren't trained to hate situations like that, because they are. For starters, you never know whether the client is taking the investment ideas you provide and building up his or her own portfolio while you get bupkus in commissions. (As you probably know, commissions have been on a downtrend since the Ford Administration. A retail broker will get something like 40 percent of the actual commission revenue generated, but commissions are far lower than they were even just a few years ago.) The worst case is when the client's outside portfolio is in fact much bigger than the full-service portfolio, although, as a practical matter, the people we're talking about would all have a couple million with Rutherford & Hayes, minimum. Hey, we're not completely stupid.

But I should admit that we're not that smart, either. You see, it was perfectly legal for Koenig to *try* and sell the shares he thought he owned. He presumably gave the sell order through his discount brokerage firm, which then contacted what we call the custodian bank, which actually holds the shares in question. Only this time they weren't holding anything, so they couldn't deliver the shares to whoever bought them from Koenig. That's when Koenig cried foul.

As long as the muckety-mucks at Rutherford & Hayes believed Koenig's story, they had no choice but to buy shares in the open market, and give them to him so that he could complete his phantom sale. For all practical purposes, Rutherford & Hayes was "short" PLX Technology, which was a lousy place to be. When you're short and a stock keeps going up, your losses are unlimited. If R&H ended up buying at the peak, they paid something approaching $50 a share for PLX, then turned around and gave it to Koenig for $25 per share. Never mind the gruesome details. Suffice it to say that Kyle Hooperman managed to lose $25,000 on a $10,000 investment by unwittingly or carelessly going short. (As to whether Koenig was making up the whole story, I can't say. But it's his word against Hooperman's, and if he won that matchup while Hooperman was alive, I'd say he's destined to win it forever.)

By the way, the two IPOs that Shari Beck mentioned were big, big winners, just as she said, er, bragged. (Not to be cinical, but it's my experience that people have very selective memories when it comes to the IPOs they've invested in. You only hear about the good ones.) Both stocks popped at their initial offerings, which, as I recall, came sometime in the late spring of 1999. That's what Internet IPOs were supposed to do, basically because people bought them indiscriminately. The problem was that, believe it or not, the market actually did discriminate—eventually. Investors soured on content providers like TheStreet.com, and it didn't help that the company shifted from a subscription-based business model to one based on online advertising revenues. That type of uncertainty never plays out well. The stock fell from 70 to 12. Priceline didn't fare quite as badly, but it dropped from its post-IPO hype price of 165 all the way to 60 before it recovered. It turns out that investors were worried that the company's early successes with cheap airfares and hotel rooms couldn't easily be transferred to other product lines, at least not with a respectable profit margin. I guess you could say that investors started naming their own price for Priceline shares. Any way you slice it, if she's bragging about how much money she made with those two stocks, I assume she didn't hold either one of them very long.

Personally, it doesn't sound as if someone as well off as Shari Beck is going to kill Kyle Hooperman because he lost her fifteen grand, but you never know. Maybe her son Eric doesn't take those losses in stride. Let me know when you get something on him.

Your not-so-famous shamus,

Cliff.

P.S. I know perfectly well how to spell "cynical," but I figured that as long as we're in America, our e-mails should have a spelling error or two.

Cliff found himself thinking that Philip Marlowe managed to solve cases perfectly well without e-mail. At least Trace's little notes were getting better. The usefulness of this particular one remained to be seen, but at least there weren't any 85-year-olds.

But why the stuff about the stupid book? Cliff had a vague memory of *This Is Not Your Father's Stockpicking Book*. It explored the connections between the stock market and things like weather, advertising, the media, and other more or less daily facets of our lives. It was a decent enough book, but hardly a world beater. It wasn't even as funky as it sounded. The weather chapter wasn't about sunspots; it was about how companies react to climatological changes, and how irrigation companies could benefit in 1989 from a drought in 1988. About the only thing Cliff remembered was that funny things could happen with funny weather. Banana companies such as Chiquita gained when their crops got destroyed early in the cycle, because the increase in prices more than made up for the decrease in volume. But when the crops were destroyed late in the cycle, after harvesting, all they had was a bunch of rotten bananas, and Wall Street wasn't nearly as impressed. Common sense, really.

Cliff couldn't help but think of Neal Miller, the one Fidelity manager whom absolutely no one has heard of, and also the one with the best record. Miller was no stranger to weather-related choices. He once bought shares of Barefoot, the fertilizer company, as a drought recovery play. Early in his tenure at the New Millennium Fund, he emphasized his eccentricity by declaring that his investing was "inferential, not linear." Conveniently, no one knew what he meant, but the translation was that he was more interested in the trend of a business than with price/earnings ratios. Even if a company traded at 50 times earnings, Miller would hold on as long as the company's business momentum continued, figuring that the market would always pay more for better-than-expected results, even from a lofty starting point. So it was no coincidence that, in his peer group, he was one of the most aggressive in loading up on Internet stocks. Later, it became no coincidence that he obliterated that same peer group in performance, especially in 1998 and 1999. So maybe Milton Koenig was trying to learn the same tricks, all in the privacy of his own home.

Just for kicks, Cliff logged on to Amazon.com to look for the book. It was out of print, so it would take at least a couple of weeks to get a copy. Not that Cliff really wanted one. According to Amazon, *This Is Not Your Father's Stockpicking Book* came out in 1995, so it was way too early for Internet plays. It probably didn't even mention that "El Nino" was an anagram of "online," a little-known connection between two of the biggest buzzwords of the '90s. And a lot of the other stuff in the book was outdated—the eventual fate of just about all stock market books.

One item caught Cliff's eye, though. More specifically, something *didn't* catch his eye, even though he was looking for it. According to the Amazon database, the book never came out on tape.

CHAPTER 9

Winter was going but not quite gone. A light, puffy snow fell like confectioners' sugar on the Manhattan sidewalks, disappearing with every footprint but coming back for more. By seven o'clock it was already dark, not to mention damp and chilly, and New Yorkers were starting to snuggle in for the evening. Millions of conversations, discussions, rehashings, and arguments had yet to unfold.

And at the Boar's Head Tavern, Maude the barmaid still wasn't getting the point.

"You mean like Ricky Martin?"

"Not exactly," Cliff said. "That was a media blitz. I'm talking about when something or someone pops up again and again by complete accident."

"Got it! Joey Buttafuoco!"

"Uh, not that kind of accident," Cliff said. "Look, here's what I mean. A year or so ago, my ten-year-old niece happened to mention that she got the role of Sacagawea in her school play."

"Sacka what?"

"Sacagawea. She was the young Indian girl who served as a scout for Lewis and Clark. You know, the pioneering advertising agency."

Maude wrinkled her forehead. "Cute, honey. Very cute."

"Hey, it's worth giving out misinformation every once in a while. You never know who you're going to face on Final Jeopardy." Cliff grabbed a handful of filbert nuts and sent a big smile her way. "But the whole point is that you're not *supposed* to know Sacagawea. My niece had to remind me who she was. It's the type of thing ten-year-olds know and adults have forgotten, sort of like sedimentary rocks or the capital of Gabon."

"Tell me about it. I can't even remember how to make paper mache," Maude said.

"Anyway, no more than a week after I heard this Sacagawea name for the first time in thirty years, I was channel hopping, and damn if I didn't come across a PBS special on the Lewis and Clark expedition. And then, just a few days after that, the Postal Service announced that it was putting Sacagawea on a new stamp. Three times in ten days, right out of the blue. Now I ask you. Shouldn't there be a name for that sort of thing?"

Maude said, "Around here we just call it a co-inky-dink."

Cliff was looking for a more specific label for the phenomenon. "Sacagawea syndrome" was a mite clumsy, but it would have to do.

The latest installment of the syndrome came from 3-D Live. If it hadn't appeared on Kyle Hooperman's computer screen on that fateful February night, Cliff might never have been the wiser. But it did, and he was. That night marked the beginning of 3-D Live's fall from grace. Now, just two weeks later, Cliff happened to catch the Dow Jones newswire reporting that the company's earnings were going to have to be restated sharply downward. Trading was halted at noon, and the stock didn't reopen all day. A very ominous situation. Which was why Cliff was glad to see Lou Battaglia push his way through the revolving doors in front. Lou didn't seem happy. He trudged toward the bar at a pace that was considered slow even in pallbearing circles.

Lou was a senior analyst at Rutherford & Hayes, specializing in the entertainment sector, but at this point in his career he felt more senior than analyst. He'd made a few good calls in his day—he was named to the prestigious *Institutional Investor* all-star team for being bullish on Disney at precisely the right time. Lou had pointed out that Disney's market capitalization wasn't much higher than the value of its real estate, and that higher ticket prices would be readily absorbed by the public, meaning that the company had the operating leverage to produce substantially higher earnings. It was a brilliant and timely call. The only bad news was that it came in 1984, and you can't go on reputation forever, no matter how popular that thought might be on Wall Street. Lou was about 60 now, balder and pudgier than Cliff remembered. His cheeks looked particularly puffy, as if he was taking tuba lessons. Most of all, he looked lost without his cigar, but such was life in the smoke-free Big Apple.

"What'll it be, sweetie?" Maude asked.

Lou managed a wry grin, like he was the Tin Man and hadn't used his smiley muscles in a while. "What the hell, Cavanaugh's paying. Make it a banana daiquiri."

"Make it two," Cliff said. "Can't let my old friend Lou drink alone tonight."

Cliff took a gander at Lou's posture, which resembled the famous back from Notre Dame: Hunch. Cliff motioned toward the one remaining window booth. Lou was only too happy to plop himself down.

"Good old Boar's Head Tavern. Used to be my second home, you know." He seemed almost sentimental. "I can't believe Fluffer put this place on his hit list. Guess it's too seedy for him."

"I think it can do just fine even without Sean's patronage," Cliff said. The Boar's Head was no one's definition of swank, but it knew how to make the best of a sweet location. Judging by the prices of the drinks, everyone at the bar was a Salomon Brothers arbitrageur.

"It's worse than that," Lou said. "Let's just say that if you're ever caught taking a client here, you better be able to prove it was the client's idea."

"Is that right? So the good ship Cummings is seeking new ports?"

"As always."

Cliff peered out the window and looked up at the mosaic of bright lights coming from the office building two blocks up the street, chez Rutherford & Hayes. "Who knows? Maybe Cummings bought the Hubble telescope and is peering in on us right now."

Just in case, Lou flipped a bird toward Fulton Street.

"Well, you know the R&H way," Lou said. "Rules and more rules, but as soon as a client wants something, the rules change. You bend over backwards until they stick you. . . ."

"Ahem," Cliff interrupted. "A damsel approacheth."

It was Maude, carrying two banana daiquiris in wide-rimmed glasses you could land a Frisbee in. "Here you go, fellas. Drink hearty."

It was going to be a long night.

■ ■ ■

"All I can say is, I'm sorry."

"No need to apologize, Lou. I don't own the damn stock."

"Yeah, I know. But I had to apologize to someone. I've been too busy scratching and clawing to admit that I just plain blew it." Battaglia had been a visible backer of 3-D Live since it came public, and if he had ever changed his mind, he kept it all to himself.

By now, Cliff knew the 3-D Live basics. The company was dreamed up by a mad scientist type named Hubert Stanislaw. Stanislaw's inspiration came when he noticed that fans of professional basketball teams would meet at their home arena to cheer their team on during the playoffs, *even for an away game.* All they got was a big screen, some camaraderie, some concessions here and there, and maybe a group appearance on live TV when the game was going their way. But that was enough. College students whose schools were in the NCAA basketball tournament did much the same thing. But because there was no actual game at the arenas in question, admission was free. Stanislaw figured he could do even better.

There was already something called Jumbotron, which drew big crowds by broadcasting all sorts of sporting events on a suitably located big screen. But Stanislaw's idea was more futuristic. His vision was to beam a three-dimensional version of a team's away game directly onto its empty home court. That way, instead of looking at a big TV, you'd take advantage of the existing space to create a game that looked like the real thing, only with holograms instead of human beings. The crucial difference is that you could charge real admission, on top of the same concessions a real game would bring. And there were plenty of new worlds to conquer after basketball. He envisioned soccer riots in two stadiums instead of just one.

But Stanislaw's futuristic bent didn't stop there. Even as he and his fledgling firm toiled on the artificial intelligence that would make his dreams come true, he added another vision. The second phase of the business started one day when he visited a neighborhood health club. As the story goes, he was appalled by the waste. All he saw were people pedaling on bikes that stayed still, climbing stairs that went nowhere, and lifting weights only to put them right back down again. Why not put all of this energy to good use? Stanislaw figured that if he harnessed the proper technology to these various machines, he could provide enough electricity to pay the club's utility bill three times over. And so it was that ActivEnergy, a fully owned subsidiary of 3-D Live, was born.

Both concepts struggled for years, trying to gain a real-life foothold. Stanislaw had a few early backers, but most venture capitalists had plenty of other places to put their money and avoid the risks of 3-D Live. Finally, Stanislaw decided he'd better tap the IPO market before the company's cash ran out. It just so happened that his brother-in-law, Charlie Beecher, was a broker at Rutherford & Hayes. Charlie put him in touch with the syndicate department and presto! Ten million shares at $12 apiece; enough to give Stanislaw's enterprise one last shot and Lou Battaglia a permanent migraine.

"I'm telling you, they put on a slick act," Lou said. "Stanislaw had this miniature 3-D display he took with him everywhere on the road show, and people lapped it up. The deal was oversubscribed, and it flew out the door. First trade was at 19½, and it hit 24 by the end of the first day. Not much in the Internet age, but remember, before the road show, this company was worth about five of these daiquiris, tops. The New York Exchange would never have listed it, so Stanislaw gets it listed on the American Exchange instead. That alone should have told me he was a screwball."

"So what was the peak on the stock?" Cliff asked. "Sixty, or something like that?"

"Close. 58½. And people thought it was going to 1,000. Stanislaw was talking deals with the Knicks, Lakers, you name it. You gotta understand, by signing up with Stanislaw, a pro hoops team figured it would have 82 home games instead of just 41. It was the answer to all their payroll problems. The NBA front office was going nuts. And that's when we had the goddamn meeting." Lou paused to play a bit with his maraschino cherry. "That's what you want to know about, isn't it?" he asked. "The meeting we had just before Hooperman got knocked off?"

"I'm all ears," Cliff said. Far better than something amateurish like, "Meeting? What meeting?" Putting a guilt-ridden Lou Battaglia in a wooden cubicle turned out to be a brilliant stroke. For a brief second, Father Herlihy seemed wildly overpaid.

"We had a special meeting with the portfolio managers, where we went over all our new issues,"* Lou said. "People were getting on Jeremy Nash for URLybirds, which seemed fair enough. Then all of a sudden Hooperman stood up and said 3-D Live was an accident

---

* He meant new issues as in recent corporate underwritings, not as in new psychological issues. But in this case, one led to the other.

waiting to happen. Usually they wait until *after* the accident has happened, but not Hooperman. He said I must have been getting paid off by the syndicate guys to put my name on a stock like that. Then wouldn't you know that Fred Gletz chimed in and said he had doubted the stock all along."

"Gletz? Gimme a break. If doubting grew hair, he'd be on *Planet of the Apes.*"

"Tell me about it," Lou said. "Back in 1988, Gletz said that Microsoft would never be able to keep software prices high, so no need to buy that one. And of course McDonald's and Wal-Mart were oversaturated, so forget them, too. Then he came up with the idea that Compaq wouldn't be able to keep its profits up in a world of cheap PCs. What a moron."

"Wait a minute. He was right about Compaq."

"Yeah, he was right, but he started his whole doomsday act in 1993. The stock didn't stumble until about five years later, and by that time it had gone up something like eightfold. Someday I'd like to figure out how a lunkhead like that survives in this business."

"Simple," Cliff said. "He just makes sure that all of his clients are even bigger skeptics than he is. I hear he turned down Mikey, the cereal kid."

"The real pisser is that I eventually agreed with him about Compaq," Lou said. "Do you have any idea what it's like to sit through a meeting on the same side with that waste of space? That's the problem with these meetings. After two minutes, you're not talking about stocks anymore. You're talking about all the history of everyone in the room, and believe me, everyone's got history."

"So what was Gletz's problem with 3-D Live?"

"Oh, get this. Gletz said that 3-D Live was overrated because their method wouldn't work on something like baseball, where the size of the playing field isn't the same from stadium to stadium."

Cliff thought about that one for a second. The objection wasn't entirely misplaced. He could just picture some Red Sox left fielder making an easy grab at Yankee Stadium while his hologram counterpart at Fenway Park ran smack into the Green Monster. And golf would be even more of a joke. But the point was that 3-D Live could grow twentyfold just by tapping the sports within its grasp.

"Vintage Gletz," Cliff said. "Disregard the near-term outlook and worry about some theoretical problem ten years down the road."

"I should have done the opposite," Lou said. "The real problem was right in front of my nose, and all I was doing was looking into the future with my bogus crystal ball."

Cliff knew well the futility of the crystal ball approach, especially in a country whose successes included Dial-A-Mattress and *Dr. Quinn, Medicine Woman*. You just never know what's going to stick.

"So where are we right now?" Cliff asked.

"In the crapper," Lou said. "The technology doesn't work."

Cliff worked hard not to spit his daiquiri on Lou's lap. "What do you mean it doesn't work? Since when?"

"Since about 11:48 this morning. That's the shit that hit the fan today. Modern artificial intelligence just isn't ready to beam people onto floors, no matter what it says in Hubert's sales literature. We're looking at thirty million in R&D down the toilet."

"And the contracts they signed?"

"Gonzo. Hence the earnings restatement."

"Next thing, you're gonna tell me that they were already booking the revenues even without the cash."

Cliff took a look into Lou's eyes, which, strangely enough, looked a lot like Andre Agassi's—down triple match point.

Cliff said, "I was joking."

Lou said, "I know. But it's exactly what happened. Cliff, you can stick a fork in the goddamn stock. It's done."

It was obvious that Lou had committed a big no-no by recommending a company whose accounting was that generous. Most R&H clients probably didn't realize that a company can report current earnings even without any real revenues, just by prorating a long-term contract they *think* looks solid. But that's different from actually being solid, and it was Lou's job to sort all that out.

Analysts aren't supposed to fall for accounting scams. When a company reports its earnings, an analyst takes nothing at face value. If a company's sales were flat but earnings went up because of a slashed advertising budget, an analyst is supposed to notice. If a company ships product early and books the revenue to meet Wall Street's projections for the quarter at hand, an analyst is supposed to ask what's going to happen in the *next* quarter. When a media company spreads its costs of acquiring new subscribers over four years—even though the average subscriber skips out after only two years—an analyst should be calling "Foul!" because a write-off surely looms.

But Cliff also knew that Lou knew all this and more, and the last thing he needed was a reproachful look at a time when the damage was already done.

"Do you think Hooperman knew that the 3-D stuff didn't work?" Cliff asked.

"Funny you should mention that. At first I thought it was just another one of his hunches—you know, like McDonnell Douglas."

"Yeah, I remember that one," Cliff said.

"Except that the more Hooperman talked, the more it sounded like he had been doing a little homework. He was dropping names of people at the MIT Artificial Intelligence Laboratory—the AI, he called it. He was talking about polarization and a whole bunch of technical terms he had just picked up. He explained that Stanislaw's little box was literally a smoke-and-mirrors technology that some researcher had dreamed up. It was just a bunch of translucent stick figures. No way could it be built on the stadium-size scale that the company was talking about."

"Yikes," Cliff said.

"There's more," Lou said. "Hooperman was also nice enough to point out that the people 3-D Live was using to demonstrate their energy conversion capabilities were world-class athletes in peak physical condition. He had the figures to show that normal people couldn't generate enough electricity to make the investment worthwhile. You see, Cliff, I think Hooperman wanted the whole table to know that anyone who knew how to dial a phone could have gotten the same information."

Lou kept shaking his head and swirling his cherry around in his drink.

"The real irony, Cliff, is that I was telling all this stuff to *Moneyline* on the night Hooperman was killed."

"You were on *Moneyline?*" Cliff asked.

"That's right. The stock had just started to tank, and they wanted to know what was up. I had been following the company longer than anyone else, so they invited me in. If you want a tape, I made one when I got home."

Cliff chuckled. He knew the show perfectly well. CNN had taken an adventurous step by teaming Stuart Varney and Willow Bay. He was a seasoned financial reporter best known for his erudite accent, and she was a sports anchor best known for co-hosting *Inside Stuff* with Ahmad Rashad. *Moneyline* didn't attain on-air chemistry until the Union Carbide/Dow Chemical merger, but it had gotten better with time. Cliff sometimes tuned in at 11:00 to catch a repeat of the 7:00–7:30 program—the time slot that Lou would have appeared on live.

"No thanks, Lou. But I'm glad to hear you've got an alibi."

"I didn't know I needed one," Lou said. He pulled away from the table ever so slightly.

"You didn't," Cliff said. "But that was before I found out about Hooperman dragging you through the mud like that. What did you say to him?"

"Nothing."

"Nothing? He sets out to embarrass you in front of all your colleagues and you say nothing?"

"Cliff, I didn't have to say a word. Jeremy Nash told him that if he didn't shut up he was gonna kill him."

CHAPTER 10

Jeremy Nash popped up abruptly when he heard Cliff's knock, as if he had been caught playing "Donkey Kong" on the computer screen in front of him. But all the screen offered was an array of numbers that was presumably part of his job. "Spreadsheet: The Game" had never caught on.

"Sorry, I wasn't quite ready for you," he said. "I can't believe it's five-thirty already."

"It's 5:25," Cliff said. "Sorry about that." He took a step inside the office and then stopped momentarily. "I suppose this isn't the time and place to say that the *early bird* catches the worm."

Nash excused the lame play on words. "You got that right."

If you sent an NYPD sketch artist over to Midtown Actuarial School, you'd get a pretty good likeness of Jeremy Nash. Short brown hair, mustache, silver-chrome glasses. Twenty-eight years old, if that. Bright-eyed and bushy-tailed. A navy tie with thin yellow stripes, set against a white button-down shirt. If it was July, the shirt would be short-sleeved, in the tradition of all numbers geeks, past and present.

But a good Wall Street analyst has to do a lot more than merely crunch numbers. Endless curiosity must come with the territory, along with skill in asking questions. From what Cliff had heard, Nash had those attributes in spades. Only this time Nash was the one with the answers, before Cliff even asked a question.

Nash said, "Look, the syndicate guys leaned on me and I caved. That's pretty much the whole story on URLybirds."

When it came to URLybirds, Nash was between the proverbial rock and a hard place. Either he confessed to having marginal ethics by pumping a stock he knew was tainted, or he denied any ethical wrong-doing—which left you wondering about his analytical skills. He opted for the ethical transgression. Cliff wasn't sure what his preference said about the state of the analyst kingdom, but it said something.

Actually, Nash was trying to have things both ways. By his way of thinking, his "recommendations" of URLybirds shouldn't have fooled a seasoned investor. There was an unusual candidness about risk factors, and even his bullet points (Profitable Internet play, Unique business format) seemed to damn the company with faint praise. Nash felt protected. He knew that analysts rarely get fired for touting their own firm's merchandise, so it was easier not to make waves. Plus, the firm's clients typically blamed the *portfolio manager* when something went wrong, not the analyst.

Nonetheless, the fact remained that the URLybirds research reports had Nash's name on them and they said BUY. That much he couldn't deny. Except that, by this time, he was more interested in denying something else.

"Listen, Cliff, about me threatening Hooperman and all that. It was just something that I said in the heat of battle."

"So when you said you'd kill him, you didn't really mean that you were gonna kill him."

"That's right."

Cliff put the fingertips of his left hand to his forehead and started shaking his head. "C'mon, Jeremy. Who do I look like, Lieutenant Tragg?"

Jeremy looked perplexed, and Cliff quickly realized that there may have been more suitable analogies at his disposal. It was a generational problem. There are Internet analysts and there are people who watched *Perry Mason*, and never the twain shall meet.

"Lieutenant Tragg was the guy who arrested the people that Perry Mason took on as clients," Cliff said.

Nash still seemed perplexed, perhaps even more so. He took a look at his spreadsheet, as if it held the answers.

"Don't you understand?" Cliff asked. "Practically every one of Mason's clients had threatened the victim at some time or another. It always came up in the courtroom scene, and it was very good theater and all that. But every last one of the clients was innocent. An arrest warrant from Tragg was like a 'Get Out of Jail Free' card."

"Someone should have told me sooner," Nash said.

Cliff said, "I tell you what, Jeremy. Suppose you tell me what you were doing the night Hooperman was killed. Then I'll forget all about any threats you might have made his way."

The phone rang and Nash was all over it. Saved by the bell.

The caller was from one of R&H's satellite offices, presumably on the West coast. Even to a listener at only one end of the conversation, the subject matter was obvious.

"I wouldn't worry about that," Nash said. "I don't think the government wants all the top Internet companies to set up shop in Bermuda."

They were talking about Internet sales taxes. The absence of sales taxes on online purchases was a constant gripe of conventional retailers and a constant source of concern among Internet investors. Many people assumed that states would find a way to collect their taxes, but that wasn't Nash's position. At this point, he was more worried about the financial health of local governments than he was about the threat to "his companies," as analysts like to call the things they study.

Nash looked Cliff's way and held up his index finger, suggesting that he'd be ditching the call as soon as he could. Cliff looked around the office and realized that Internet analysts didn't have the same sort of tchotchkes that other analysts did. Consumer products analysts had their product samples. Transportation analysts had their little model trucks. Jeremy Nash needed a few such perks to jazz up the place.

After hanging up, Nash took out an envelope from his desk. He opened it up and took out a couple of rectangular slips of paper. "See these?" he asked.

"They look like tickets," Cliff said.

"Not just tickets," Nash said. "Springsteen tickets. You asked what I was doing the night Hooperman was killed, and here's your answer."

"Wonderful," Cliff said. "If only Springsteen had been playing that night, you'd be in the clear. But you really should rip the tickets in half. Much more believable that way."

"Cliff, the concert isn't for another month. The reason I'm showing them to you is that while Kyle Hooperman was getting himself shot, I was buying these tickets on eBay. I was right here at my computer."

Ah, the old eBay alibi, Cliff mused.

Online auctioneer eBay was one of the great efficiencies of nature, not to mention one of the truly great stories in the annals of e-commerce. The company pioneered the creation of a global system to sell the stuff that would otherwise end up at an estate sale or a flea market. Floor lamps. Snuff boxes. Model trains. It was also one of Jeremy Nash's most prized stock selections. He seemed a whole lot more interested in talking about eBay than he had about URLybirds.

Cliff was reminded of Tim McCarver, the acclaimed baseball announcer who did Mets games in addition to national post-season broadcasts. Whenever McCarver came up with a good insight, Cliff made sure to hit the "Mute" button, lest he hear the same insight five times before the inning was over. There was no "Mute" button available in real life, which was too bad, because Cliff knew most of the eBay story. But he had to admit that, in the investment business, hearing one good idea a thousand times is much better than hearing a thousand bad ideas one at a time.

The entire premise behind eBay was that the company got a cut of everything bought and sold on its site. Which is not to say that eBay made any real money, at least not in the twentieth century. System development costs were sufficiently high to eliminate near-term profits. Reported earnings could be managed by the way in which the company accounted for its stock options. But Nash saw the possibilities. He was pushing the stock as soon as it came public in 1998. He saw it go from 10 to 230 by the spring of 1999, at which point its market capitalization was a sprightly $30 billion.

That's when Nash took a slight misstep. A report he issued gleefully noted that eBay was worth more than the New York Times, Gannett, and the Tribune Company combined. He felt the comparison was appropriate because online auctions had the potential to completely undo the market for classified ads, a major revenue source for newspapers—as if newspapers weren't facing enough competition from the online world already. Nash pounded the table, insisting that clients get out of newspaper stocks, even though he wasn't the one covering them. It was a major violation of protocol.

Worse still, Nash was off the mark. Newspapers weren't done yet, not by a long shot. In the summer of 1999, they were getting a big boost from a recovery in national advertising, especially in important categories such as autos and telecommunications. On the expense side of the balance sheet, newspaper companies were benefiting from sharply lower newsprint costs. If that weren't enough, companies such as the New York Times and Gannett were getting positive contributions from other media businesses, notably from their ownership of various radio and TV stations. Nash had overlooked the fact that corporate earnings often revolve around more than a single variable. His doomsday scenario regarding classified advertising was woefully premature, and in the investment world, being early is the same as being wrong.

Making matters worse, eBay began to tank. The stock swooned in the summer of 1999 as the whole Internet sector took a breather. The breather got worse for eBay when system outages forced the company to close its site on a couple of occasions. Investors got antsy. The stock dropped some more. But that's when Nash stepped in and became a hero all over again. He argued that the system-related panic was a buying opportunity, in the "when bad things happen to good people" mold. And he was right. The stock quickly snapped back from an interim low of $88 to over $150 within a couple of months. And, this very afternoon, CBS MarketWatch was spreading the word that Yahoo! and eBay were in talks about some form of business combination. Nash said he had released a memo explaining why an outright takeover was unlikely, but he clearly was enjoying the ride as eBay shares traded north of 200 on Instinet, the after-hours electronic trading network.

Nash had enjoyed a similar success a couple of years before, when the AOL system was having trouble keeping up with subscriber growth and the result was erratic if not downright lousy service. When R&H portfolio managers got scared and needed Nash's assurance, he sat them down and quoted Yogi Berra on the subject of a trendy restaurant: "No one goes there any more. It's too crowded." Managers got the point and held on. It worked for AOL, and it worked for eBay, too. No wonder Nash was held in such high esteem. Brash Nash, they called him. R&H's newspaper analyst still hated his guts, but everyone else loved him.

The irony on Cliff's mind was that, ordinarily, you wouldn't expect a company like eBay to provide an alibi. Technology was known for destroying alibis rather than creating them. Cell phones were renowned for enabling people to do things that were never possible when communication was tied down to an actual line. And adding a simple tape recorder to "The Hound of the Baskervilles" might have thwarted Sherlock Holmes forever.

Even eBay had a "proxy" system that enabled people to put in bids without actually being present when the auction ended. That's why Nash was so specific about being at his computer. Online auctions have an expiration date and time. You can place a bid anytime you want, but if you're not vigilant, you run the risk that someone else will outbid you by $5 and slip a bid in with literally two seconds to go. So, as long as Nash was on the level, he was holding the tickets to his innocence in his right hand.

"I don't suppose you'd let me use the other Springsteen ticket."

"Not a chance," Nash said. "But it just so happens that a few of us are going to the Knicks game tonight. Care to come along?"

"Who're we playing?"

"The Rockets," Nash said.

The Rockets were a team that Cliff could relate to. Their average age was the highest in the league, almost AARP material. This might be the last chance to see Hakeem Olajuwon in action. It was already too late for Charles Barkley, who had blown out his knee in the fall. Maybe the Knicks would be giving him a send-off party. That would be fun. Better still, it might be an opportunity to hook up with some of the R&H regulars. There was no law preventing a murderer from attending a basketball game.

Wishful thinking.

"Count me in," Cliff said.

CHAPTER 11

The trip from R&H's offices to Madison Square Garden is an easy ride on the #2 uptown express, almost as if the whole line was curved crosstown just so Wall Streeters could make it to the games on time. And unlike the East Side uptown trains, the #2 train has the courtesy to stop right at Fulton Street.

The train that picked up the R&H crew had started out at Flatbush Avenue, once a mecca for the old Brooklyn Dodgers' games at Ebbets Field. By the time it had stopped at Wall Street and then at Fulton Street, it had collected its fair share of financial types, but traveling at seven o'clock still beat the hell out of rush hour, especially in March, when the heating system hasn't yet recognized Mother Nature's own efforts to warm the city up. Rush-hour subway rides in March are clammier than the night shift at Van de Kamp's.

The walls of the car had a thick coat of carmine paint that gave an antique feel to the whole experience. So did the station stops. After Fulton Street came Park Place, the Monopoly namesake. Then it was on to the West Side turn at Chambers Street. The names of the downtown stations were spelled out in little bathroom-type tiles—one of this old subway system's few charms. Somewhere after Chambers Street, Gletz poked his finger into Cliff's side.

"Pssst," he said. "I think that's Marilu Henner."

"Where?"

"Over there. Under the Devine and Fallows ad." Devine and Fallows were personal injury attorneys who liked to advertise near construction sites and in fast-moving public transportation. Almost directly underneath their toll-free phone number was a brunette in an Armani suit. Red highlights, 50 going on 43. And Gletz was staring at her like she was gonna smile back and give him some tips from her latest diet book.

Bad move. Women riding by themselves on New York subways don't smile. They just stare at their magazines or newspapers like they're cramming for the LSATs.

Cliff looked in the opposite direction until he saw the woman's reflection in the subway window, and he didn't move his eyes even after she looked up. For some reason, the same women who loathe head-on ogling don't seem to mind if you bank it off the glass. She let herself be looked at for a few seconds, smiled, and then returned to her magazine. She didn't happen to be Marilu Henner, but she seemed nice enough, just the same.

It wasn't long before the train reached 34th Street—Penn Station. The Penn Station complex had housed Madison Square Garden since 1968. Ever since then, a monsoon could hit the city and fans could still make it to a Garden event nice and dry. The Knicks were world champions in 1970 and 1973, but they hadn't won the title since. The closest they came was the 1998–1999 season, when they miraculously made it to the finals but lost to the San Antonio Spurs.

Two days ago, they had played the Spurs in Texas, with the same result.

If you like escalators, Madison Square Garden would be your kind of place. The Rutherford & Hayes box, like all of the Garden's skyboxes, was at the very top of the arena, a far cry from Spike Lee's first-row digs. But the R&H box was never intended to house the city's biggest sports fans. It was a place to take big clients, prospective clients, maybe just whiny clients. The vertiginous ones could watch the game from any one of several TV screens in the comfy, carpeted confines of the skybox. Dinner was prepared in a kitchenette in back.

As Cliff entered the room, he thought he detected a faint aroma of beef teriyaki. But he wasn't expecting any free samples, for one very good reason.

"Cavanaugh, is that you?"

It was Sean Cummings.

"Guilty as charged, Sean." And if being Cliff Cavanaugh was a crime, there was no way to get off as a first-time offender.

The lay of the land was a skosh out of the ordinary. Behind Cummings was a couple in their 40s who were overdressed just enough to place them in the prospective client slot. The man wore an ascot scarf, à la Klaus von Bulow. Chatting them up was Phil Aarts, who headed the online brokerage division at R&H. The implication was clear: This couple wasn't about to sign on until they had some reassurance about the firm's online capabilities. And whoever they were, they had enough assets to get the heavies interested.

Cummings said, "I'm a little surprised to see you here, Cavanaugh. You know, in the middle of a case and all. You really think Patrick Ewing had something to do with this?"

"Everyone's a suspect as far as I'm concerned," Cliff said. "I'll try and get the game ball dusted for fingerprints."

"I didn't think whoever killed Kyle left any fingerprints," Cummings said.

"They're all over the murder weapon," Cliff said.

"I didn't think the murder weapon had been located."

"Details, details."

Cummings said, "Well, if you wanted to talk to me, I think you could have found another time and place."

"I figured you'd probably come here to get motivation from the spirit of Charles Barkley," Cliff said. "At least Barkley made it through the SEC without a hitch."

It was an inside joke. Too inside. Cummings might not have been aware that, in some circles, SEC stands for the Southeastern

Conference. Barkley had played in the SEC while at Auburn. But the only SEC that Cummings ever cared about was the Securities and Exchange Commission, the official arbiter of the financial community. He moved closer. Close enough for Cliff to know that the beef teriyaki guess was right on the money.

"Listen, Cavanaugh, you can zip it as far as the SEC goes. Other than Kyle Hooperman's occasional indiscretions, our shop has been as clean as a whistle. You understand?"

"Is that why Hooperman never made it to the institutional side?" Cliff asked. "Because of 'indiscretions?' "

Cummings said, "Come on, Cavanaugh. You know as well as I do that Kyle Hooperman was a great investor, but he was also a royal pain in the neck."

"So his error account was officially in the discomfort zone?" Cliff asked.

"Nice guess," Cummings said.

"I pride myself on my guesswork," Cliff said. "Can I also guess that the SEC is almost through with its investigation?"

Cummings shot a glance toward Mr. and Mrs. Ascot Scarf. Phil Aarts had their full attention. He returned his stare to Cliff.

"All I can tell you is that if the SEC finds anything on anyone who's still here, that person's gone by sundown. You got that?"

"Is that what happened to Hughie Szabo?"

"Szabo was a bad apple," Cummings said. "Our clients have been better off ever since he got canned. Better prices all around."

"Is Szabo better off?"

"He was a thief," Cummings said. "He was skimming clients' accounts and he got what he deserved. And that's all I'm going to tell you."

"Aw, shucks. Things were just getting interesting."

"Like I said before, this isn't the time and place." Cummings was trying to whisper, but by this time he was giving the Knicks' PA announcer a run for his money.

"Hey, Sean. Settle down. You're right. You're absolutely right. What do you say we watch the game?"

Telling Cummings he was right was more soothing to him than the Brahms lullaby. Besides, Cliff didn't see any point in going further.

Not after checking out Cummings's nose.

Even from the interstellar vantage point of the skybox, Madison Square Garden was a special place to watch a basketball game. Cliff looked out across the arena and saw the list of Knicks players who had had their numbers retired: Dick Barnett, Dave DeBusschere, Earl "the Pearl" Monroe, Willis Reed, Walt "Clyde" Frazier. There was even #24, Bill Bradley, who had been in the news for different reasons.

Today was supposed to have been a big day for Bradley. It was primary day in a slew of Southern states, notably Texas and Florida. But one week before, Al Gore had won everything in sight on "Super Tuesday," forcing Bradley out of the race. Today Gore was sewing up the delegates that would put him over the top. And just as New Yorkers love a winner, they don't take much of a shine to losers. Bradley's defeat was filling the whole arena with negative karma.

The game taking place in the background started out on a dull note. The elder statesmen of Olajuwon and Ewing were being given the ball as a matter of professional courtesy, but they weren't doing much with it. At the midway point of the first quarter, the game was tied, 6–6.

Cliff caught a glimpse of Fred Gletz. Gletz watching a basketball game was a study in abject dilettantism. His knowledge of the game didn't extend much beyond double dribbling, so his only alternative was to obsess with the score. When the Knicks got behind, he tensed up. When they pulled ahead, he breathed easy. Every emotion seemed exaggerated for effect.

Cliff recalled that an enterprising young financial writer had once charted the ups and downs of a basketball game in an effort to show their similarity to the ups and downs of the stock market. The comparison wasn't completely in jest. Both endeavors were characterized by small incremental movements that had the potential to create big cumulative swings. And the psychological elements were similar. The crowd was the most silent at those very moments when the Knicks were in the biggest trouble—even though, by definition, the best parts lay immediately ahead. Traders had to endure the same irony every day—investing when they felt the worst, and selling when they felt great. No wonder traders didn't last long. Better to be in it for the long haul and not panic when you get down. Cliff shot a glance at the Knicks' bench. The occupants were cool and calm, even businesslike. No panic at all. Maybe because they knew they were better. Meanwhile, Gletz was chewing his nails and swigging from what appeared to be a flask of Jagermeister.

Then there was Phil Aarts, an up-and-comer who happened to be at the right place at the right time. Rutherford & Hayes had toyed with online trading for years, but Aarts happened to be the guy who made the push when the barriers were breaking down. Online trading was a controversial subject in the world of full-service brokerage. The business model of the full-service broker revolved around holding the clients' hands, making them feel good, maybe even making them money, and meanwhile getting top dollar for commissions.

The business model of the online broker was entirely different. No expensive real estate. No research staff to pay for. Without costly overhead, these brokers could compete on price in a big way. For the same trade that a full-service broker might once have charged $250, E*Trade could come in at $10 or less. Same for DLJ*direct*, Ameritrade, and dozens of firms vying for online supremacy. It was only a matter of time before full-service clients everywhere would wake up. The stock market seemed to understand the shift that was going on. Early in 1999, Charles Schwab passed Merrill Lynch in total market capitalization, even though its revenues were one-eighth the size.

Schwab had trouble holding its lead against its own set of competitive pressures. Ironically, although the company had built its name by promoting the advantages of discount brokerage, aggressive traders, lured by those advantages, were now setting up secondary accounts with brokers whose commission structures were even cheaper than Schwab's. Throughout this mess, the one undeniable trend was that online brokers as a whole were gaining accounts. Of special concern to people like Sean Cummings was that firms like Merrill Lynch and Rutherford & Hayes were losing brokers. To the old-line brokers, quick-change artists like Phil Aarts were about as welcome as a turd in a punch bowl.

"Phil, how're you doing? Cliff Cavanaugh. I think we met last year during the playoffs."

"Oh, sure. The Miami series, right?"

"Yep. So how's business?"

"It really blows the mind," Aarts said. "The floodgates have opened." Aarts had a chiseled face that suited his reputation as a Young Turk. His chin was a trifle too long, and his thin nose could easily fit in the smallest opening, even as doors were being shut in his face.

"How are folks like Gletz taking to the changes?" Cliff asked.

"Gletz is hanging in there. He's given a few of his accounts to Charlie Beecher, just to help us get started."

The process of revving up the online division involved a tithing process not altogether unlike an expansion draft in baseball, or even in basketball. Investment managers pointed amenable clients toward online accounts, then maybe tossed in a couple of hand-picked ones for the good of the firm. Maybe.

"How about Kyle Hooperman? Was he warming up to online brokerage?"

If Aarts was surprised by the direction of the conversation, he didn't show it. "Cliff, I'll put it this way: Kyle wasn't exactly high on our donors list. Cummings and I tried to make him see the light, but he wasn't interested in helping out."

Houston swished an 18-footer and the crowd went wild. It was Allan Houston, the Knicks' point guard. Even Gletz lightened up a bit. It was midway through the second quarter, and the Knicks led, 33–25. By halftime the lead had been pushed to 45–34.

There was no sign of Mr. Ascot Scarf and his wife. It wasn't unusual for prospective clients to leave after the first half. The real fans called them "walkies," and not because they walked out. The term was a carryover from the 1950s, when people who were trying to be hip bought *one* walkie-talkie. It was vaguely possible that the visitors had retired to a nearby sports bar to pick up the game on TNT, but Cliff wasn't betting on it.

They ended up missing a pretty decent game. New York's lead was reduced to a single point several times in the fourth quarter. They pushed it back up to five, but Knicks' guard Chris Childs got called for a foul and Marcus Camby picked up a goaltending violation—on the same play. It was 70–69. Ewing and Latrell Sprewell took charge down the stretch, and the Knicks went up by six, 79–73. Houston's Steve Francis then hit a three-pointer to cut the lead in half, and Cliff smiled in Jeremy Nash's direction. Nash picked up the reference immediately. Francis had lost a tooth in a game against Denver three weeks earlier, and the Houston fan who found it immediately put it up for auction on eBay. Nash's favorite company was now the tooth fairy.

Houston came no closer. Olajuwon ended up 0-for-9 from the field, and the Knicks won, 91–85. The evening was a success. Then again, it would have been a success even if Ewing had clanged all his free throws and the Rockets had won at the buzzer.

That's because, judging from Sean Cummings's funched nose, something fishy was going on at Rutherford & Hayes.

CHAPTER 12

The snow of the prior evening was a false alarm. It had given way to one of those bright, crisp days that March owns the rights to, at least in the northern hemisphere. The noonday sun was bearing down on Cliff and Trace as they made their way past the lunchtime shopping crowd. Their destination: Rockefeller Center skating rink. To watch, of course, not to skate. Seven-eighths of the rink was taken up by preschoolers taking their first strides toward the Anaheim Mighty Ducks. It was a serious case of too many men on the ice.

"Better enjoy it, kids," Trace said to the air above the rink. "The season is almost over."

"And none too soon," Cliff said. He took a deep breath. "Ah, I can feel it coming. How does the poem go? 'In just, spring. When the world is puddle-wonderful.' "

"e.e. cummings," Trace said. Softly, as if she didn't believe it. Her eyes opened a bit wider. As she nodded approval, she made one of those expressions that turns a mouth into a crescent moon and a chin into a peach pit. "I'm impressed, Cliffie. Can't say as I was expecting you to know that one."

"Of course it's e.e. cummings and of course I know it. Just applying the knowledge I acquired during brokerage training."

"Yeah, sure. And the word 'gullible' isn't in the dictionary—right, Cliffie?"

"No, I'm serious. Well, sort of serious. I mean, you're right. You don't need to know the first thing about fine arts to become a stockbroker. But along the way, you do learn the fine art of making people think you know more than you really do."

"I don't think that's brokerage training. I think it's called the American dream," Trace said. She tilted her head and let her face bask in the sun.

"All the more important to do the act right," Cliff said. He was making a palms-down motion with his hands, fingers spread apart, like he was Seiji Ozawa telling the orchestra to go adagio.

"First, you survey the topic at hand and pluck out only those details you feel comfortable with. Then, just as important, when you feel yourself reaching the absolute end of your rope, you quickly change the subject without anyone smelling a rat." He now spread his hands in triumph.

"And we unsuspecting folks accord you with knowledge you never had?"

"Precisely. So if I'm at a party and people are talking baseball, I can let it slip that Ty Cobb had a lifetime average of .367. Maybe I'll even throw in that Ted Williams came in at .344. Then I head off to the men's room. Some people are gonna conclude, 'Wow, that Cavanaugh is something. He knows the batting averages of anybody who ever played the game.' "

"Yeah, I guess they might," Trace said.

"They do it more often than you'd think," Cliff said. "It's called the extrapolation principle, and it works like a charm."

"So you don't know the next line of the poem?"

"Not a clue. If I did, I wouldn't have stopped."

Actually, the poem that *was* on Cliff's mind came from an old *New York Magazine* contest, circa 1980. The challenge was to come up with a four-line stanza ending with a pun on a famous person's name. His favorite entry went something like this:

The temperature is thirty-eight
An in-betweenish day
I do not know my snowman's fate
It may not Mel Torme.

The entry only got second place, which was highway robbery.
First placewent to a lesser construction that must have charmed
the judges because it ended with Tutankhamen. King Tut was big
back then.

The day at hand felt a tad warmer than thirty-eight degrees. At
least it was warm enough to go without gloves, which was something
of a relief to Cliff as he unwrapped the tinfoil from his falafel sand-
wich. Getting the tahini sauce on your bare hands was bad enough,
but getting it on leather gloves was downright disgusting. Trace had
ordered a couple of Mountain Dews to go with the sandwiches, an
inspired choice. It came in cans, so you didn't have to look at it, and
it went surprisingly well with the falafel. Cliff had tossed in a slice of
baklava for his dessert.

Trace said, "I guess I'll just tell my mother I was treated to an ex-
otic midtown lunch by a gentleman who insisted on reciting poetry
to me."

"Not bad, but make it a *dashing* gentleman," Cliff said as he took
another chomp on his falafel. "No need to fib when you can lie outright."

"Okay, dashing gentleman, what you're telling me is that Lou
Battaglia blew it, right?"

" 'Fraid so." Cliff made a loud sigh. "Right now, he considers himself the sloppiest analyst on the Street. And knowing Lou, he's pop-
ping Prozacs like they were Flintstone vitamins."

"Aw, c'mon. There has to be a way to cheer him up. Misery loves
company. Tell him Christiaan Barnard left his forceps in a patient's
ribcage, or something like that."

"It's more insidious than that," Cliff said. "Lou's problem was that the market was basically telling him what a great job he had done, which pretty much guaranteed that he wouldn't recognize his mistake until it was too late. Besides, he wasn't the only analyst to get caught up in 3-D Live. Just the only one with any sense of shame."

"So what happened to the stock this morning?"

"It opened at 15, down 21 on the day. Your basic 60 percent drop."

"And Lou is still recommending it?"

"Nah, he had already bailed out yesterday afternoon when the stock was at 36, but it's not as if anyone could have gotten out there. Analysts just do that to save face. When your sell trigger is the news that the company's product doesn't work, you're too late by definition."

"Product? I thought 3-D Live had a whole different part to its business," Trace said. A mouthful of pita bread did nothing to hold back her question barrage.

"They do," Cliff said. "The health club power generation part— ActivEnergy, or whatever it's called. But investors decided that the hologram stuff was sexier, so that's what they've been focusing on."

"Geez. I thought the market was supposed to be all-seeing and all-knowing."

"Only in the academic journals," Cliff said. "They'll tell you that, at any given moment, all the publicly available information about a company is woven into the price of its stock, or some horseshit like that. What they don't tell you is that the market can have worse tunnel vision than Mister Magoo."

"A 60 percent drop is pretty bad tunnel vision," Trace said.

"Yeah, 60 percent isn't exactly what we call a narrow trading range," Cliff said. "I don't mean to say 'I told you so,' but I've never much cared for companies that are divided into two unrelated parts. I could give you twenty reasons why I don't bother with them."

"Twenty reasons; is that so?" Trace looked at Cliff for a half second longer than he would have liked. If he hadn't just finished his lunch, he would have eaten his words.

She folded her brown lunch bag flat and took out a green felt-tip pen from her handbag. "Here you go, Cliffie. Use the other side if you need to. But remember, I have to be at Cloud 9 by 1:30."

Cliff wondered whether it was too late to insert a "no giggling" clause in Trace's contract. Cloud 9, by Carol Churchill, was the latest Mainstage production. At this moment she was living up to it better than he was. He took the makeshift stationery warily, as if the napkin inside the bag had turned into a water moccasin. But the jig was up. He pulled the napkin out and moistened it on the outside of his Mountain Dew can, a poor man's Wet-Nap that was essential after his falafel-and-baklava combination plate. He wiped off his hands, then stared at Trace as he took the cap off the pen. At the top of the bag, right under the Union Camp logo, he scribbled as follows:

Reason #1: The market has two chances to freak out instead of just one.

"That's what I was just saying happened with 3-D Live," Cliff said. "Got it. One down, nineteen to go."

Cliff kept writing.

Reason #2: Result of bogus acquisitions.

"Do you happen to remember a company called CML Group?" Cliff asked.

"Sounds vaguely familiar," Trace said.

"They're better known as the company behind NordicTrack."

"As in the medieval torture chamber my folks stuffed in their attic, am I right?"

"I guess you know how the story ends," Cliff said. "But believe it or not, they were going great guns for a while in the early '90s. That's when they bought the Smith & Hawken garden catalog business." Cliff paused for effect. "You're supposed to ask why they would make such a nonsynergistic acquisition."

"That's almost spooky, Cliffie," Trace said. "I was just going to ask why in the world they would make such a nonsynergistic acquisition."

"Because they had cash to put to use, that's why. That's the trap. When a product like NordicTrack is flying off the shelves, cash can build up."

"And this is a bad thing?" Trace looked confused, like she had just read the last panel of "Zippy."

"Cash buildup wouldn't be a bad thing if people bought a new NordicTrack every year," Cliff said. "Because then the company could, in theory, put the cash back into its business and make even more money. But when companies can't do that, they get edgy. They know that the return on their excess cash is basically limited to whatever they can earn in a money-market account. So they figure that if they want any prayer of maintaining their earnings trend, they have to go out and buy *something*. So they go out and buy whatever strikes their fancy."

"They should have bought MCI," Trace said. "Roman numeral companies should stick together."

"Well, they were only about $30 billion away from pulling that one off," Cliff said. "The problem is that once a company adds a second prong out of nowhere, even if things go well, analysts find the combined company harder to follow, and the stock often doesn't command the premium it used to. Can I make that reason number three?"

"Sure, why not? I'm feeling generous."

"Generous, my ass. You know I'm leaking oil."

Cliff distinctly heard another giggle as he jotted down his latest entry.

Reason #3: A two-part company is only as strong as its weaker link.

"I think I can squeak out one more from this same setup," Cliff said. He kept scribbling.

Reason #4: The halo effect.

Cliff said, "Maybe the worst part of all is that you have stupid investors who ask questions like 'I wonder whether that superb CML management team can pull another winner out of its hat with Smith & Hawken?'"

"Isn't that a natural question?" Trace asked.

"Yeah, it's natural, all right, but so is the rhythm method. Personally, I'd rather be safe than sorry."

"I don't get it," Trace said. "What's the danger?"

"The danger is the entire premise that the company's management skills can be transferred onto a completely different product line. Think about it. The only thing investors really know about management is that the company made money. Which, being shareholders, they think is wonderful, right?"

"Check."

"So the only real question is whether the good times can last, right?"

"I guess so."

"But we just saw that when a one-product company goes on the acquisition trail, it usually means that it's running out of reinvestment opportunities in whatever business made it successful in the first place. That's a sell indicator right there."

"But—."

"Hold it, Trace, I'm on a roll. I mean, wouldn't you think that CML shareholders would thank their lucky stars that NordicTrack caught on and made them money in the first place? I'm not knocking Smith & Hawken, but isn't it pretty dumb to suddenly get excited by garden supplies just because they got bought out by a company that had success in exercise equipment?"

"So why do people do it?"

"It's human nature," Cliff said. "We can't stand to close on a high note."

"I thought investors were taught to buy low and sell high."

"Oh, we're supposed to, all right, but it doesn't work that way in real life," Cliff said. "In real life, CBS thinks *AfterMASH* is a terrific idea, and Larry Holmes fights until he's 80."

"You've got a point, Cliffie."

"Damn straight I do. Leaving on a high note is un-American."

Cliff was momentarily distracted by the sound of one of the city's mounted cops clomping down 49th Street on his chestnut steed. Looking up, Cliff realized that about twenty bystanders were getting some degree of amusement out of his animated investment lecture. Despite all the talk about the glut of investment information out there, it was Cliff's experience that no one ever seemed to get enough. Even the horse, now reined in close to the group, seemed to be taking it all in.

"Is it 1:30 yet?"

"It's only twenty of one."

"How long does it take you to get back to NYU?"

"Twenty minutes," Trace said. "Slightly less if I skip the whole way back."

Cliff stood up in a flash, as if the Queen Mother had just walked by.

"Look, an osprey!" He pointed the green felt-tip pen high above 49th Street.

Trace looked at him cross-eyed. "Cliff, if an osprey had come to Rockefeller Center on its lunch hour, one of those little kids down there would be in its claws right now."

"No osprey?"

"No osprey, Cliffie. Maybe just a really, really overweight pigeon."

"I'm not gonna make it to twenty, am I."

"Doesn't look that way," Trace said. "But I'll let you off the hook. As far as I'm concerned, all you really need is *one* good reason. Even four is overkill."

Cliff felt a trifle patronized, but Trace was right. Most good investment decisions are made for one good reason rather than four little reasons trying to masquerade as one big one.

"Actually," Cliff said, "The more I think about it, what's happening right now at 3-D Live is basically the reverse of some of the patterns I've seen."

"How so?"

"Well, for one, 3-D Live was a split-personality company from the beginning, as opposed to getting that way through acquisitions."

"And is there a *number two* this time?" Trace's giggle was now slightly out of control. Officer Dibble would have considered it disturbing the peace.

Cliff said, "Yeah, and it's an important one. With 3-D Live, there's actually an *anti*-halo effect. Which is a way of saying that, right now, it doesn't matter what's going on at ActivEnergy. The market has decided that anything with so much as a whiff of Hubert Stanislaw on it is dogmeat."

Cliff closed the cap on the pen. He grabbed his lunch bag and took a ten-foot hook shot toward the trash receptacle. The shot clanged off the rim. He put in his own rebound before a certain mounted policeman could dismount.

"And one more thing," Cliff said. "You were able to pick up the clubs?"

"Yep, got 'em."

"Good. That should make life a whole lot easier. You want a few pointers?"

CHAPTER 13

Few things in life are certain, but Trace would have wagered the Clintons' legal fees that she would never, ever wake up at 6:30 A.M. for a game of golf. Not minigolf, not Microsoft golf, and certainly not the real thing. Of course, that was before she wanted to get in a word with the reclusive Erwin Sparks, Jr.

Sparks was no longer a client of Rutherford & Hayes; he had pulled his account just two weeks after Kyle Hooperman's murder. But his lifestyle lived on. He headed his own options trading firm, and he was known to allow himself a few indulgences. Legend had it that early each morning, weather permitting, Sparks could be found getting in a brisk eighteen holes at a private country club in Darien, Connecticut. If ever there was a time and place to speak with him, that was it.

The drive to Darien was easy enough, and the spiked golf shoes gave Trace a heavy foot on the gas pedal. Better to be headed out of the city than the other way around. The scenic route was via the Merritt Parkway, but Trace didn't have time for that. She headed up I 95 instead. She observed a mental moment of silence upon passing Exit 20—Rye, New York, home of the late Kyle Hooperman. From there, it was ten minutes' drive to the Greenwich tolls, then ten minutes more along the Connecticut panhandle to the Darien exit. The scene along I 95 was uninspired, industrial, and billboarded. It didn't begin to tell the full story. Some mighty nice real estate was tucked in the nearby woods. It was a great place to buy your dream house, as long as you could outbid the chairman of Kidder Peabody and Ivan Lendl.

Darien seemed pretty sleepy as Trace exited the interstate, but she couldn't be sure how fast Erwin's clock was running. Internet directions came in handy at a time like this. Gas station attendants wouldn't necessarily know the way to the Wee Burn Country Club, and they wouldn't necessarily like being asked. According to Cliff, the club's name came from a golfing term. A burn was a winding type of water hazard; a wee burn was a small one.

She took a right on Middlesex, and within seven-tenths of a mile she saw the sign she was looking for: Hollow Tree Ridge Road. The name was too long to fit on the brightly painted mailboxes that Trace whizzed past. The boxes were either solid red or solid green, as if by town ordinance. The numbers, painted in a crisp white, were a Helvetica font. It was a beautiful country road. Trace resolved to stay under the speed limit on her return trip.

Within a few minutes, she arrived at a three-road intersection, behind which was the Wee Burn parking lot. It was 8:05; maybe too late, but maybe not. She screeched her rental car into a parking spot as if auditioning for Domino's. From the back seat, she took out the golf bag containing the clubs that had belonged to her grandfather in the days when woods were made of wood. No matter. They were just for show. To match her lightweight green golf jacket, Trace was wearing one of those white-and-green, hole-in-the-top golf visors you see on the LPGA tour. Her hair was bunched in a ponytail and popped up like a shaving brush at the back of her head. The capper was a white culotte that deliberately clashed with the March landscape and common sense.

No one was in sight. She hoisted the golf bag's strap onto her right shoulder, hustled past the clubhouse, and cut through the employee parking lot, which was, conveniently, right next to the eighteenth green. She got a ball and threw it into one of the three sand traps in front of the green. She took out her pitching wedge, set the bag down away from the green, the way Cliff had instructed her, and began flailing away. By the time she got the ball onto the putting surface, she was working on a double bogey. She stashed the wedge and took out her putter.

Moments later, she caught a glimpse of a man in an orange sweater and white pants, walking toward her on the eighteenth fairway. If her background research meant anything, the man was Erwin Sparks. Then again, it could have been Y.A. Tittle. It was hard to tell; he was still some distance away. Whoever he was, he stopped, took a club from his bag, and stopped again. Trace eventually realized that he wasn't going to play until she putted out.

Trace tapped at the ball, not nearly hard enough. Or so she thought. She hadn't noticed that the green was at a slight angle. The ball kept going to the lip of the green, approximately five feet from the sand trap she had worked so hard to get out of. Then she remembered one of Cliff's tips: If you can't sink the putt, at least make sure the other guy *thinks* you sank it. She putted again, this time uphill, and the ball came to rest about eight feet in front of the cup. Now it was a piece of cake. She tapped another putt, knowing that the man in orange was too far below the hole to see what was going on. She picked the ball up three feet from the pin, palmed it, and plucked it from the cup like Harry Blackstone pulling a silver dollar from a spectator's ear. Three-putting made easy, by Cliff Cavanaugh.

Trace walked to the side of the green, slid her putter in with her other clubs, picked up her golf bag, and waved up to the man in orange. She then took out an imaginary scorecard and wrote her imaginary score. Realistically, she figured she would have shot about 250 for the full round, not counting the ten-stroke penalty for violating the Marquis of Queensberry rules on 18. As she was tabulating, the man's iron shot landed ten feet from the cup. Trace applauded. He tipped his cap.

As the man in orange approached the green, he was starting to fit the description that Trace had gotten from R&H intelligence. He was about 35, lifeguard good-looking. His curly blond hair was poking out the sides of his cap. He had a blond mustache to match.

"You new around here?" he asked. He seemed to have forgotten about his birdie putt opportunity.

"Brand new," Trace said.

The man strode toward her. He tipped his cap with his left hand and put out his right. It was clammier than you'd expect on a cool day, probably because he had just ditched his golfing glove.

"Pleased to meet you," he said. "Lucky Sparks is the name." A convenient solution to the "Erwin" problem.

"My name's Rosie," Trace said. After Rosie Ruiz, famed Boston Marathon interloper. It was hard to start a round on the last hole and not think of Rosie.

Trace had argued in vain that Cliff should be the one to play golf with Erwin Sparks. After all, he had played the damn game before. But Cliff insisted that men aren't interested in talking to strangers on the golf course unless those strangers happen to be women. Trace tried to counter by saying that women aren't interested in being hit on at 8:00 A.M. Whereupon Cliff said just because women aren't interested doesn't mean men won't try.

"I didn't think there was anyone on the course in front of me," Lucky said.

"Um, I only played the back nine," Trace said. "That was plenty for today."

"Well, I couldn't help but notice you struggling with your putter there," he said. "Maybe a lesson with ol' Lucky could save you a stroke or two."

"I don't think a lesson is what I need," Trace said. "I should just go away in March instead. My golf game and my stocks are heading south, so why shouldn't I?"

Lucky laughed loudly, a bit more loudly than he probably meant to. He couldn't help it. Men on the prowl aren't accustomed to women making the jokes. They don't know quite how to react. Usually they overdo it, the way Reagan did in his photo ops with that wacky Yassir Arafat.

"You in the market, Lucky? You should be. Lucky's a great market name."

"Now that you mention it, I've done pretty well for myself," he said. He was grinning ear to ear, like he'd just pulled a nine-pound bass from the wee burn.

"So you manage your own money?" Trace asked.

"Pretty much, that's right," said Lucky.

"That's too bad," Trace said. "I was looking for the name of a good advisor." She shook her head. "Maybe it's just as well. I guess we're not quite to the point where a hedge fund is going to be interested in us—right, Lucky?"

"Well, now that you mention it, some of my assets used to be managed by a downtown firm," he said.

"What's its name?" Trace asked.

"Rutherford & Hayes," Lucky said.

Trace said, "The name sounds familiar. Would you recommend them?"

The conversation was starting to sound like an EFHutton ad.

"Would I recommend them?" Lucky echoed. "That depends. Do you own any municipal bonds?"

"No, I don't," Trace said.

"Well, maybe you should. Rutherford & Hayes switched me out of Treasury bonds and into munis last year. The Treasuries were yielding 6.1 percent, but that's only 3.7 percent after tax.* My munis yield me 4.8 percent tax-free. A nice little deal."

"So why aren't you still with them?" Trace asked.

---

* In the world of Lucky Sparks, everyone is in the 39 percent tax bracket. His calculation was simply $6.1 \times (1.00 - .39) = 3.7$

"Interesting question," Lucky said. "Did you happen to see a Ferrari in the parking lot on your way in?"

"Not that I can recall," Trace said.

"Of course you didn't, and you know why?"

"I guess I'm not very observant in the early morning."

"Nope, the reason you didn't see one is because there *wasn't* one."

He stopped momentarily, just to let Trace appreciate the vacuum he was experiencing.

"You see," Lucky said, "I told my advisor I was going to cash out of this stock and buy myself a Ferrari with the proceeds, just for the hell of it. But by the time he got around to selling, well, let's just say they aren't making Ferraris at that price any more. I bought a Saab Turbo instead."

He sounded sad. Trace wondered why she hadn't seen his name on *The New York Times* neediest list at Christmastime. But there was no question that the stock in question was URLybirds. According to the records Linda Greer had provided, that was the only stock he had sold in the year 2000. And he had sold it just two days before Kyle Hooperman's murder.

"I thought most people kept their long-term investments separate from money they might need in the short term," Trace said.

"Well, pretty lady, you may be right about that, but let me tell you something. If you never sell, all you have is a paper asset, and all it can do is make you feel better when you look at your brokerage statement. I say no sense in getting liquidity if you're never going to sell."

"I'm not sure I understand," Trace said. By now she could deliver the line standing on her head.

"Let me explain it this way," Lucky said. "I know a guy who has a baseball signed by Babe Ruth. Says it's worth a million bucks. Says it was the best investment he ever made. But would he ever sell the thing? No way. Not unless all his other investments went belly up and he needed the money. So it's not really worth a million bucks, is it? That's what I tell him. But he doesn't listen. Frankly, the only thing I regret about selling is not selling *earlier*."

Lucky was just standing there shaking his head. His ball was still sitting on the green, and his birdie chances were getting lower by the minute.

"Tell me, pretty lady. If I had sold out sooner, would you have gone for a spin in my Ferrari?"

"I don't know," she said, reaching into her golf bag to pat one of her grandfather's woods. "I did bring my own driver, you know."

This time Lucky didn't laugh quite as loud. Maybe he realized that today was his unlucky day.

But Trace was thinking about something else, something pretty obvious that she had missed the first time around. Maybe Cliff had missed it, too, she wasn't sure.

What she realized was that the clients for whom Hooperman had bought shares of URLybirds were all completely different. Different ages, different investment styles, different requirements all around. The only thing they had in common was the size of their portfolios; Linda said that each one generated about $40,000 annually for Hooperman, based on the standard R&H yearly fee of one percent of total assets. But size was irrelevant for stock selection, wasn't it? After all, if you were running two aggressive portfolios and one was ten times as big as the other, you could buy the exact same stocks for both accounts. As long as you kept the ratio of each purchase at ten-to-one, the two portfolios would be functionally identical.

So why did all these clients happen to own the same stupid stock?

CHAPTER 14

As Trace headed back to Manhattan, she viewed Operation Erwin as only a mild success. She had found him and she talked to him; she even got him to open up a little bit. But he didn't seem to say much of consequence. Still, on that score, the final judgment was in Cliff's hands. Cliff was the one to whom financial information was sacred, and he seemed to do more with it than most. "Never take the 'invest' out of 'investigation,' " he liked to say. Hey, it's his money, right?

The rest of Trace's morning accomplishments were even milder successes. In order, they were: (1) leaving Wee Burn without being tailed by a Saab Turbo; (2) stopping at Christy's Market and picking up an eight-ounce orange juice, otherwise known as breakfast; (3) returning the golf clubs and rental car to their rightful owners. All sorts of exciting stuff. When she finally got back to her loft, Trace found a place for her golf visor on a closet shelf, where it was likely to live out the Cenozoic era. She had all of forty-five minutes to prepare for her next mission.

She turned on the TV and stumbled across an episode of *Simon & Simon* on A&E. If it was mindless rerun fare she wanted, she had come to the right place. The Simon brothers were making the world a little safer by tracking down the killer of a sexual surrogate. Jameson Parker posed as someone who got nervous in the presence of women, which was about as believable as Ralph Kramden getting nervous in the presence of a jelly doughnut.

Somewhere in the middle of the episode, Trace came to the inescapable conclusion that Naomi Campbell does not braid her own hair. Or maybe it was just that her own hairs were antisocial — all thirty-five hundred of them. Especially the shorter strands on top, which didn't much want to mingle with the longer stuff below.

Her idea was to create a new look with which to launch the second round of portfolio manager auditions. It had figured to be a snap. Trace made about a dozen thin braids and pulled them behind her head. She secured them with one of those Native American-style leather thongs that always looked so good when Georgia O'Keeffe painted them on. The mirror had another opinion. It said, "Medusa."

Trace undid the braids and settled for a bun.

Because her hairdo wasn't close to perfect, Trace sought out an equally uninspired ensemble. She chose a gunmetal gray suit belonging to her roommate Gail. The off-the-rack number had pointy lapels and was in style sometime during the Carter Administration. Trace thought momentarily about adding some white hose, but it wasn't really necessary. The suit made any fair-skinned inhabitant into an instant albino. All she needed to complete the look was a pair of $7 reading glasses from CVS. Those who recognized her now did so at their peril.

■ ■ ■

Ginny Truesdale was all smiles when Trace arrived, which was mildly unfortunate. Close up, her teeth were a mite crooked and had a couple of gaps. Cliff's "Stonehenge" label was looking better and better. What was it about the British and teeth? Trace wondered. Apparently they'd rather be holed up in the Tower of London than visit an orthodontist's office.

Truesdale was pleasant enough, but she didn't have the Welcome Wagon act down quite the way Lenci did. There was no one offering coffee, tea, or scones with clotted cream. The office itself was much like Lenci's, but without the clutter. A braided ficus tree stood like a big green lollipop to the left of her desk, not far from the chair that Trace perched herself in.

Truesdale was a no-nonsense type; that much was certain. She wore a wedding ring, but there were no photos of any past or present little Truesdales on display. The only personal item on her desk was a sign that read "If it can be solved by money, it's an expense, not a problem." Words to live by.

But Trace, aka Mimi Dalrymple, did have a money-related problem. The pretext of the meeting was that she was unhappy with her current portfolio manager. So, within moments of sitting down, she reached into her briefcase and brought out a brokerage statement she and Cliff had conjured up. "Take a look at page two," she said.

Truesdale pulled up her reading glasses. She wore them on a chain, the way they did at the duplicate bridge club. She carefully scrutinized the pages in front of her, which were modeled after one of Cliff's old R&H portfolio appraisals. As Ginny pored over "Mimi's" alleged holdings, Trace took another look at her hands. They were rugged-looking and crying to be soaked in Palmolive. They had no fancy nail polish or anything like that. No nails, really. Perfect for squeezing the trigger of a Colt Government Model .380, assuming she wanted to.

But what Cliff was especially interested in was Ginny's investment style, not her physique. He was convinced that people revealed a lot about themselves by the way they invested. Fred Gletz, for example, wasn't a good suspect. One look at his portfolio and you'd realize that he never had an original idea in his life. Cliff figured that the only way Gletz could have committed the murder is if someone else had killed Hooperman first. But Ginny was an unknown commodity, and this was her dress rehearsal.

Appraisals are designed to show you pretty much everything you'd ever want to know about your portfolio. They list all your holdings, of course, with split-adjusted purchase prices and current prices.

Then they categorize your stocks by industry and maintain percentage breakdowns, so if you accidentally become 40 percent weighted in energy stocks, your appraisal's pie chart screams at you to diversify. In the old days, clients would receive complete appraisals at the end of each fiscal quarter, but that had all changed. What Trace had could be generated pretty much any day of the year, from online data. As predicted, page two was a standout.

"Oh, my. I see what you mean," she said. "If my advisor had placed me in 3-D Live shares, I might be looking for a replacement as well."

"So you don't own the stock?"

"I have never owned the shares and I never will," Truesdale harumphed. The news wasn't a big surprise. There was something profoundly American about the company's underlying concepts, even if its founder was born in Transylvania. But the real root of her distaste was a risk factor.

"I don't purchase shares of an unproven enterprise with a gearing of 20 percent," Truesdale said.

Trace would have preferred English. Fortunately, she was well prepared. She reached once more into her briefcase and pulled out a one-page British-English financial dictionary that Cliff had jotted down for her. There were more entries than she was expecting. "Turnover," for example, was Brit-speak for "trading volume," as on an exchange. "Gearing" meant financial leverage, otherwise known as debt. A gearing of 20 percent meant that the company's financing was 80 percent debt and 20 percent equity.

She recalled Cliff's pointing out that leverage isn't always the worst thing in the world. If you bought a house for $400,000 *in cash* and sold it a year later for $500,000, you made 25 percent—before paying the laundry list of ancillary costs that invariably accompany real estate transactions. If, instead, you put $100,000 down and took out a $300,000 mortgage with monthly payments of $3,000, your return on investment would be in the neighborhood of 50 percent.

Of course, if you raised the mortgage rate a bit, or extended the period of ownership, or lowered the final sales price, you could drastically lower the final return figure, because the payments would be no bigger relative to the whole transaction. Which is basically what Hubert Stanislaw was experiencing. He was apparently pouring money into 3-D Live's far-flung visions without first cleaning up the company's balance sheet. Without an established revenue stream, the debt was too much to handle.

"I should also warn you," Truesdale continued. "Now that the company's earnings have disappeared, the price/earnings ratio listed on the appraisal is no longer valid." She rolled the "r" at the beginning of ratio.

Trace started to play a bit with her bun. "You know, I hate to admit it, but I don't really have a clue what a price/earnings ratio is." She was about to explain to Ginny that the Schwab ads always faded away before actually explaining the concept, but she thought better of it.

Truesdale didn't miss a beat. "It's quite simple, really," she said. "It's the price of a share divided by the earnings per share." She returned her eyes to the pages in front of her. "I see that you have H&R Block priced at $40 per share. Its earnings for the last 12 months were $2 per share, so its price/earnings ratio is 20, just as it says on your appraisal."

"Is that good?" Trace asked.

"All things being equal, a low number is better than a high number. The idea is to buy as much growth as you can for as small a P/E as you can."

"That's all there is to it?"

"That's essentially right, yes."

Trace was beginning to understand why Cliff put price/earnings ratios on his list of the most overrated stock market inventions of the twentieth century, right between Joe Granville and Elaine Garzarelli. Cliff's theory was that the secret to the P/E's fame was in its name. Put a descriptor like "ratio" on a very simple concept, and most of the free world will be frightened by it and assume that it holds the answers to all the questions they can't answer.

"But you can't use P/Es if a company is losing money?" Trace asked.

"I'm afraid not, at least not right away. Even if the concern* is making a very small amount of money, you have a problem. A P/E of 10,000 is quite conceivable mathematically, but it isn't of any practical investment value. And I have to be honest. The most useful price/earnings ratio is usually the one based on *next* year's earnings, not this year's. That's why we have a team of analysts to make reliable forward-going estimates. If you aren't good at estimating earnings, the P/E won't have much value."

"I see," Trace said.

Ginny said, "Believe it or not, most of the companies I invest in have rather high price/earnings ratios."

"But I was always told that high P/Es meant high risk," Trace said. "I thought you didn't like risk."

"I abhor *operational* risk," Ginny said. "But *market* risk is something I'm willing to deal with. That's the type of risk that the stock market rewards you for taking on."

"So let me get this straight. You don't buy low P/E stocks?"

"Just because shares are cheap doesn't mean they're good," Ginny said.

Trace rechecked her little lavender notepad, otherwise known as her Cliff notes. The issue of cheap versus undervalued was something Cliff loved to harangue about. He addressed the same topic somewhat differently. His notes read, "If it's cheap real estate you want, start at the Love Canal." His point was that anybody can create a list of low P/Es and therefore invest in cheap stocks. Whether

---

* "Company," according to Cliff's mini-dictionary. As in "going concern." And the way their concern was going. . . .

the market rewards this practice is another matter, especially when so many companies have deserved their low valuations. A little farther down was another aphorism in the same general area: "A value investor is someone who invests in shitty companies and prays."

"Do P/Es help in identifying takeover candidates?" Trace asked. The question came out abruptly, like she hadn't been listening to much of what Ginny Truesdale had been talking about.

"My dear girl, have you no idea how out of fashion that investment style is?" Except that it sounded more like "Midea gull. . . ." Every few words, Truesdale's natural accent fought for recognition.

She went on to talk about the bygone days of the 1980s, when leveraged buyouts and hostile takeovers were daily events. And how junk bonds were used to finance transactions in which a company could be bought out and its assets sold to pay for the cost of the acquisition itself. Companies with statistically cheap stock prices had to adopt sophisticated defenses in order to thwart unwanted suitors. "It was the devil's way of saying that the stock market was undervalued," she said.

Trace wasn't a market historian, but she knew that she hadn't heard the word "undervalued" in quite some time. Where the overall market was concerned, she knew there had been a bad patch in 1990, right before the Gulf War, and another bad patch in 1994, when there were bunches of interest-rate increases. But the market hadn't been called undervalued since the release of Windows '95.

"I don't mean leveraged buyouts," Trace said. "I just think that if a company is attractive enough for me to own a piece of it, it might be just as attractive for someone who wanted to buy the whole thing."

"Well, that sounds entirely more reasonable," Truesdale said. She was well aware that acquisitions had become more strategic in nature, triggered more by the target company's business fit with the acquirer than by its cheap share price. Cases in point: AT&T/Telecommunications, AtHome/Excite, AmericaOnline/Time Warner.

Trace said, "I guess I like takeover investing because of a great tip I learned from Barbara Woodhouse. Do you remember her?"

"I'm afraid I don't." Ginny Truesdale mustered up something that was supposed to pass for a smile. "The only Barbara Woodhouse I know of used to train dogs for a living."

"Yeah, that's the one," Trace said. "She specifically advised not to use newspapers for puppy training. One of the best investment tips I've ever gotten."

Ginny Truesdale didn't have a ready answer.

"Don't you see?" Trace said. "I was one of the people who *did use* old newspapers. Every once in a while, they'd open up to the business section. All I saw were the stocks I had thought about buying, at much lower prices. It was sickening."

"Forgive me, Miss Dalrymple, but I'm afraid I don't see the connection."

"Please, call me Mimi."

"Very well, then."

"The connection is that when you invest in takeover candidates, you'll win some and you'll lose some, right?"

"Correct. That's true of any investment strategy," Ginny said.

"Right, but in this case the stocks you miss out on are, by definition, companies that have been taken over. But once they get taken over, they don't appear in the newspaper anymore, so you never have to see them again."

Trace caught Ginny Truesdale taking a glance at the clock on her desk, no doubt wondering whether this particular client was going to be worth all the trouble. She maintained her decorum throughout Trace's babbling. They managed to get in about ten more minutes of chit-chat before the show-and-tell session had run out of gas. The good news was that Trace was going to be able to spell out Ginny's investment preferences with unusual precision. She was headstrong, forthright, and good at what she did. More in the Hooperman mold than Lenci, that's for sure. The bad news was that she didn't know what it all meant. But that, as usual, was Cliff's problem.

"Here are my coordinates," Ginny said as she handed Trace her business card. "Coordinates" wasn't covered in the dictionary, but its meaning was clear. Ginny's coordinates were things like her phone, fax, and e-mail. Trace took it as "Please call us, but we won't call you."

"Miss Dalrymple, I'd like you to meet my associate, Linda Greer. She'll show you out."

Linda Greer was in her early thirties. She had sandy blond hair with extra-tight curls, like she had gone slightly overboard with the Milk Wave Lilt. She was one of those women whose lipstick seems to bond with their skin and not wear off. Today's shade was burgundy. She wore a light blue suit that showed off a few years' worth of aerobics classes. It was dressier than you might expect for an assistant, but presentation was apparently part of the job. Vanna White, without the letters.

Trace followed Linda along a plain white corridor that appeared to be the back way to the elevator bank. It was just long enough to require some small talk.

"So, have you been working with Ginny long?" Trace asked.

Linda laughed. "It's okay, Trace, we're out of earshot. I know who you are."

"I was afraid of that," Trace said. "I think I owe you about twenty favors by now."

"Catch Kyle's murderer and we're even," she said. "Anyway, they put me with Ginny to try and ease the transition. She's still got an assistant she brought over from PaineWebber, along with about ten dozen clients."

Trace had become aware that the money management game worked in that fashion. In the vast majority of occasions, the allegiance of a client was to the manager, not the firm. From the client's perspective, the manager *was* the firm. So if the manager left for another firm, any administrative hassles the switch might create were small potatoes compared to the major inconvenience of trying to find a new manager. The old firm might try to retain the clients, but most firms knew it was a losing proposition.

Trace and Linda were now stopped just in front of the back door to the elevator bank. Trace said, "Ginny just told me she came over because Rutherford & Hayes gave her more freedom to manage money."

"And you believed it?"

"Are you saying I shouldn't have?"

"It's no real secret, Trace. Ginny came over here because PaineWebber did almost no new issue business. I think she wanted to go where the money was. Brokers make almost twice the commissions on new offerings as they do on normal trades."

"Is that right?" Trace said. She felt some relief at being genuinely ignorant, as opposed to the ditzy profile mandated by her new-client act. "So it wasn't the team of Rutherford & Hayes analysts making accurate earnings estimates a year in advance?"

Linda pressed her burgundy lips together but still couldn't stifle a laugh. "The analysts play musical chairs from the day they begin till the day they retire," she said. "Let Mimi visit some other firm two years from now. I'm sure she'll bump into some R&H alumni. Except now they'll be talking about the superiority of their new firm, and they'll say it from the bottom of their hearts."

Linda opened the door to the elevators. Trace bade adieu. "Cynicism with a smile," she thought to herself. She wondered: Would she have to conduct these interviews for the next two years?

CHAPTER 15

Sometimes clues are obvious. Sometimes they are obscure. At other times, they sit in front of you for weeks without saying a word, just waiting to be discovered.

It was March 17, St. Patrick's Day. When Irish eyes are smiling and all that. But the weather wasn't cooperating. It was literally going to be raining on the Fifth Avenue parade—unless it snowed, that is, which was a distinct possibility. As for Cliff, his morning started out in an all-too-familiar way. After a power breakfast of Grape Nuts and orange juice, he turned on his AST Advantage to get the obligatory morning feed. The stock market would no more break for St. Patrick than the Flat Earth Society would celebrate Columbus Day.

In fact, the market was open pretty much every weekday imaginable. The only exceptions were Thanksgiving, Christmas, New Year's Day, Martin Luther King's birthday, President's Day, Good Friday, Memorial Day, July Fourth, and Labor Day. The market didn't shut down on St. Patrick's Day unless you happened to be in Ireland. Which reminded Cliff of an old joke. Q: Why did investors start buying Irish stocks? A: So their money could keep Dublin.

It would pass for funny until something better came along.

This particular day was the third Friday of March, otherwise known as triple-witching day. It was one of four times each year when derivative instruments such as options, index options, and futures contracts expired on the same day. Investors with memories of the '80s recalled crazy price swings as a result as institutional investors' adjusting their common stock positions in accordance with the behavior of these other instruments. But SEC intervention served to spread out the expirations and thus dampen the volatility. Cliff noted that a lot of day traders started in business with the hope of striking it rich every triple-witching day. In the words of Aerosmith, dream on.

The market was up by something like 20 points, a number that by itself said absolutely nothing. For all Cliff knew, Hewlett-Packard could have been up four points, with the other 29 stocks in the average unchanged. That alone would cause the market to be up 20, because the Dow is calculated by adding up the prices of all 30 Dow stocks and dividing by a number — imaginatively called the divisor — that gets readjusted whenever a Dow company splits its stock or a substitution is made in the average itself. For the moment, the divisor was just over 0.2, so dividing by the divisor was equivalent to multiplying the point change by five. The full, eight decimal place divisor — 0.20145268 — was a number too fleeting and too obscure for even Trivial Pursuit to bother with.

Whatever the market was doing, at least it wasn't giving back its gains of the day before. The Dow had gained 499 points on Thursday, its biggest-ever single-day point gain. Blue chips and interest-rate sensitive stocks had pummeled the Nasdaq for the first time all year. There was finally some hope in the air, even if the clouds were gray.

Cliff spent the morning victimized by his own curiosity. He started researching a company called Gumbegone, the latest prospective IPO from the syndicate department at Rutherford & Hayes. He couldn't stop, mainly because it was a neat little story. The company had come up with a new method of removing gum from sidewalks. No harsh, toxic chemicals. Just a quick application of heat, a jet of water, plus one simple scrape, and in five seconds' time a little black gum blob was gone from the streets forever.

Gum is something that New Yorkers see every day without really seeing it. The first person not to see it takes a big chunk of it home but the residue stays on the walkways and soon gets darkened by a combination of pedestrians' soles and extraneous city grime. A visitor from outer space or Utah might wonder who decorated New York's sidewalks with little black circles. Over two million on 34th Street alone, by some estimates.

Numbers like that made Gumbegone a more viable enterprise than most people had estimated. Besides, if the IPO went through as planned, the company would become the first pure play for pathological gumophobes. Prior to the year 2000, their only investment option was to short Wrigley, perhaps explaining the absence of gumophobes in the Forbes 400. Wrigley was one of those low-tech stocks that was never cheaply priced but always seemed to chug along just fine, appreciating 750 percent in the '80s and 280 percent in the '90s. That's what no debt, a market leadership position, and international expansion will do for you. The year 2000 wasn't starting out quite as well, but Gumbegone investors were rooting for Wrigley to at least hold its own, because Wrigley would be making most of the gum that Gumbegone would be removing.

Cliff liked the idea behind Gumbegone, but he found a few strikes against the investment. One was that its revenues were largely dependent on securing contracts within the notoriously fickle world of municipal governments. Not every city administration feels passionately about the need to remove black blobs from the sidewalks. St. Patrick's Cathedral on Fifth Avenue was a sooty black church for decades until the city finally sandblasted it back into a white church. Some people liked the black church better. What Gumbegone needed was a whole bunch of cities that felt consistently adamant about gum removal. Of course, they couldn't be too adamant, either. In Singapore, careless gum disposal is a criminal offense, rendering Gumbegone superfluous.

As Cliff thought about it, he realized that Gumbegone's basic problem was that it might be too effective for its own good. Even if it branched off into the seemingly fertile halls and playgrounds of the public schools, revenues were likely to be nonrecurring. Once a superintendent of schools had ponied up for a Gumbegone unit, that would be it. No repeat business. Sadly, there was no way that the company's earnings stream would ever be as reliable as Wrigley's.

Cliff's personal tug-of-war was brought to an abrupt end by the sound of *Hawaii-Five-O.* A few weeks before it hadn't been ringing at all. Now Cliff was worried about paying residuals. A female voice at the other end asked if he was Clifford Cavanaugh. Cliff acknowledged that he was.

"Will you hold for Leslie Peterborough?"

Stupid question. Leslie Peterborough was the president of Century Advisers, one of the classiest money management firms in town. Leslie was the grande dame of the financial district. She even had seniority over Muriel Siebert. If Leslie wanted to talk, then talk is what you do. Cliff hastily pulled up Microsoft Word, as if to bury his research pursuits. Leslie Peterborough was certainly not calling to get his views on Gumbegone.

"Mr. Cavanaugh, I'm told that you are conducting an investigation into the murder of Kyle Hooperman."

"That is true," Cliff said.

"Were you aware that our firm had offered Mr. Hooperman a job just two weeks prior to his murder?"

Boing! Cliff wedged the phone between his shoulder and chin. His fingers instinctively popped toward the keyboard, trying to create some semblance of a transcript.

"No, I wasn't," Cliff said. He felt capable of typing and talking at the same time, but his conversational skills sometimes suffered. His typing wasn't so hot, either. He scrawled out "Hoop—Ptbrgh job," and reminded himself that he wasn't abbreviating Pittsburgh.

"I'm glad that it wasn't common knowledge, Mr. Cavanaugh. We certainly tried to keep it under wraps. I don't need to tell you what an extraordinary addition Mr. Hooperman would have been for our firm." She spoke in a quick, clipped tone, as if she had an egg timer by her phone.

"Kyle was a phenomenal money manager, no question about that," Cliff said. He idly wondered how many of Century's existing managers would have welcomed the new arrival. But that wasn't where Leslie Peterborough was coming from.

"What concerns me is that we tried every type of lure you could imagine," Leslie Peterborough said. "We had performance incentives the likes of which Rutherford & Hayes would never even consider, much less offer."

Cliff nodded silently. Sean Cummings's reputation for penny pinching had spread across Manhattan like encephalitis.

She said, "Now I find myself wondering whether there was something going on at R&H that I didn't know about. Kyle claimed to dislike working with his clients, most of whom he regarded as an inconvenience. You'd think a closed-end fund would be a perfect fit."

She'd said "a closed-end fund." Cliff could barely believe what he'd heard. "Pardon me, Ms. Peterborough, but are we talking about the Earhart Fund?"

Leslie Peterborough stopped short, as if she'd said more than she'd intended to. But it was too late. "Yes, we are."

Cliff typed "hly sht."

The Earhart Fund was probably the best-known fund of its kind. A closed-end fund is simply a bunch of stocks, like a mutual fund. But mutual funds, by definition, are open-ended. You can always redeem your shares at net asset value—the total portfolio value divided by the number of fund shares outstanding. A closed-end fund is different because its shares actually trade on an exchange, and the price can represent either a premium or a discount to the fund's net asset value. Investors had no assurance that they would be able to complete the round trip, perhaps explaining why Peterborough named her flag-ship fund after Amelia Earhart.

Examples of closed-end funds trading on the New York Stock Exchange included the Korea Fund and the Mexico Fund. But the Earhart Fund was one of the few diversified equity funds that remained in closed-end form. In that respect, it functioned in a similar fashion to Berkshire Hathaway, the long-time investment playground of Warren Buffett. Berkshire was a former textile company that had been transformed into a holding company for Buffett's stockholdings. If you wanted to own Berkshire shares, you typically had to pay more than what the underlying stocks were worth, but such was the premium placed on Buffett's management.

Unfortunately for Peterborough and Century, they were going in the opposite direction. Fund manager Constantine Dimitriades had enjoyed some great years, but his performance was slipping. In 1999, he had invested heavily in multinational consumer companies like Gillette, Coca-Cola, and, who knows, maybe even Wrigley. They looked like safe picks. But domestic growth for each of these companies was sluggish, and on the international front they faced a different problem: The dollar was strong, so when foreign revenues were converted back into dollars, those revenues got clipped by the currency conversion. For companies whose foreign revenues were 60 percent of the whole, this was a big deal. Worse still, investors were flocking to fast-growing technology companies and leaving the multinationals behind. Better to buy astonishing growth at 100 times earnings than plodding growth at 40 times earnings, or so the theory went. Procter & Gamble had just imploded the week before on a sour earnings forecast, and its bad vibes engulfed the entire consumer sector.

Dimitriades also slipped by buying brokerage stocks at the wrong time. Apparently, he felt that the IPO frenzy would enable firms like Merrill Lynch and DLJ to post superb underwriting results. And he was right: 1999 was a great year. Unfortunately, not only were interest rates heading up, but investors became spooked by the prospect of a price war on commissions. That fear was triggered by a move by American Express Financial Advisors to offer free trading for all accounts above a certain size—a clear indication of the competitive pressures wrought by online brokers. Even though the higher trading volumes on the Nasdaq enabled major brokers to rake in outstanding commission profits for the year, price/earnings ratios came down as investors feared that the combination of higher interest rates and permanently lower commission margins would drag down future earnings.

Even when Dimitriades was on the right track, he didn't do enough. He invested in FedEx in late 1998, on the grounds that overnight deliveries were getting a big boost from the growth of online retailing. He was right: FedEx almost tripled within the year, a terrific gain for a company of that size. But his preference for established, blue-chip companies meant that he wasn't investing in the e-tailers themselves, so the Earhart Fund lost an opportunity to make up for its missteps elsewhere.

Leslie Peterborough had seen enough. She figured that a new manager would renew interest in the fund and restore the premium it once enjoyed.

"Mr. Cavanaugh, I just can't understand why Hooperman didn't leap at our offer. And now I can't help but wonder whether that's somehow connected to his murder. I'd feel better if you could uncover something."

Cliff knew that Leslie Peterborough didn't get to where she was by displaying poor instincts. And she had a point. Century could have been the marquee stop in Kyle Hooperman's career. The Earhart Fund, no less. A free rein to invest however he wanted. Maybe he simply got cold feet even before they went cold for good. Or maybe there was something keeping him at R&H besides the Madison Square skybox and the free parking space.

Ms. Peterborough didn't have a whole lot more to say. Cliff thought for a moment about volunteering his services for the Earhart Fund, but he thought better of it. He threw a few vowels into his little document and bade her adieu.

Cliff figured he'd complete his dossier on Gumbegone with a quick Internet search on gum removal, but all he got was a list of periodontists. No matter. Gumbegone's road show was right around the corner, and he wasn't going to commit without a first-hand glimpse at the management team.

It was about then that the Dow Jones Newswire came up with its most interesting nugget of the day. Trading in the shares of an old friend—3-D Live—had been halted. The company announced a press conference for later that day. The rumor du jour was that Hubert Stanislaw was being forced out by the board of directors. Cliff took another look at his screen and his eyes popped out as if on stalks.

What Cliff realized was that the activity he was engaged in— checking on 3-D Live—was precisely what Kyle Hooperman was doing the moment he was shot. And on the screen in front of him was something he should have thought of long before—a clue that had been waiting all this time to be uncovered. There in big fat letters was 3-D Live's ticker symbol: TDL.

As in Theodore David Lenci.

CHAPTER 16

Cliff tried to get Dave Lenci on the phone, but nothing doing. The system slipped him into voice mail. After a few well-placed jabs with the index finger, Cliff heard the familiar voice of Hannah Diehl, Lenci's longtime assistant. Hannah was a master juggler of the fiber-optic variety. She could keep four clients on hold while Lenci sweet-talked the fifth one. But this time around, no such queue was developing. Hannah politely informed Cliff that Lenci wasn't there. He had joined his family at the circus.

Dave Lenci. At the circus. That's what she said.

Ringling Brothers had just gotten into town for the final leg of the annual three-stop metro-area tour. They had already performed at the Continental Airlines Arena in East Rutherford, New Jersey, and at Nassau Coliseum in Uniondale, Long Island. Circus promos were all over Manhattan. The show was a homecoming of sorts for the 24-year-old ringmaster, Johnathan Lee Iverson, formerly of the Boys Choir of Harlem. "Local Hero Brings Down the House," the news-paper ads read. Apparently the publicity was working. Dave Lenci had played hooky just to be with his loving wife and two children. Will wonders never cease.

"Can I take a message?" Hannah Diehl asked. "He should be back later this afternoon."

"No, that's okay," Cliff said. "But I've got a question for you."

"What's that?"

"Do you happen to know whether Dave has his favorites when it comes to IPOs?"

"That's some question," Hannah said.

"Yeah, sorry about that, but I don't know any gentle way to ask it. I'm just wondering whether he handles his new clients the same way Hooperman did, that's all."

"Oh, well, if you're asking about them, I think I can help you out," Hannah said. "We've only had one new issue since we took over those accounts, and Dave made sure that all of Hooperman's clients were treated exactly the same way they were before."

"What was the company?"

"Palm, Inc. You know it?"

"You could say that," Cliff said.

The question was technically a bit of an insult. Palm was the hand-held organizer unit of 3Com, and its offering was one of the year's most anticipated IPOs. The offering price was 38, and it zoomed to 165 before collapsing back to the 70 range, as investors realized that the market value of 3Com's remaining Palm shares was far greater than the market value of 3Com itself, even though 3Com planned on spinning off its entire holding within six months. The price discrepancy was known to any day trader not living in a cave, but Cliff decided not to feel offended.

"So are you telling me that no one squawked?" Cliff asked.

"That was the general idea," Hannah said.

"And the transition is complete? I mean, everyone is accounted for?"

"My, you've got a lot of questions. But yes, it's complete. There was one last stock power to process from Kyle's client list, and I filed it this morning. But Dave can clear all of this up for you better than I can. Shall I tell him you called?"

"No need," Cliff said. "I'll be talking to him soon enough."

▪ ▪ ▪

Trace had mixed feelings about coming along to track Lenci down. It was a Friday, after all, and her contract gave her an automatic out. But this Friday wasn't destined for stardom the way it should have been. With NYU on break, St. Patrick's Day at Harrington's was reduced from the biggest bash of the year to a couple of kegs of warm green beer. A little sleuthwork just had to be an improvement. Besides, she actually had some progress to report, for once.

Cliff picked Trace up in the Village. Destination: Sands Point, on the northern shore of Long Island. It was a fairly easy trip if you waited until after Manhattan had disgorged its weekly commuter diet. Cliff had left a voice-mail message warning Dave Lenci to expect some company at about 9:30 P.M. Trace was waiting at 9:00 on the dot.

"Nice wheels, Cliffie," she said. "I didn't even know you owned a car."

"A well-kept secret," Cliff said. "If you hadn't flunked the GrandAm rental, I might have let you drive it by now."

"I thought these things were renowned for safety," Trace said.

"You're thinking of Volvos," Cliff said. "Anyway, it's not you I'm worried about. If I ever let you behind the wheel of this baby, I want you to be passed by Ralph Nader in a Corvair."

As they approached the Midtown Tunnel, Cliff was thankful for their choice of starting time. The traffic was minuscule, their progress steady. He was also thankful that the city had finally gotten around to installing TunnelTalk, that magic elixir that enables radio receivers to pick up signals even while under the East River. WCBS-FM was playing "Up, Up and Away," by the Fifth Dimension, a cherished memory from the sixth-grade school bus.

Trace had ridden on a different bus. Cliff was never able to persuade her that all the great songs in the world were written between

1955 and 1980, with the possible exception of "Love Shack," by the B-52s. She reminded him that '70s music included "You Light up My Life." He countered with "You Ain't Seen Nothin' Yet," by Bachman Turner Overdrive. She said "Disco Duck." He said "Disco Inferno."

On and on it went.

Sometime after they returned to dry land, Trace said, "Before I forget, I finally got a hold of Eric Beck today."

"Eric Beck. Now there's a name I hadn't heard in a while."

"I'd given up on him," Trace said. "So as a last-ditch effort I called his mother's office to see if I could reach him that way."

"And Shari came through?"

"Her secretary came through. According to her, Shari was at a special directors' meeting at Boeing and won't be back until Monday. Something to do with the end of the strike out there. But the secretary must have gotten through to Eric, because I got a call from him about 45 minutes later. He said he had just lost his job and had drowned his sorrows with a week in Cancun, which is probably why he hadn't returned my calls."

"What was his job, being his mom's undersecretary?"

"Not quite. Until last week he was going door-to-door for the Bradley campaign."

"Geez, Eric Beck working for a Democrat. I wouldn't have called that one." Cliff estimated that four-fifths of his old well-to-do New York client base had voted straight Republican.

"Well, I don't think it's a great mystery," Trace said. "Eric went to Princeton. His parents met at Princeton. Bill Bradley went to Princeton."

"I get the drift," Cliff said. This particular presidential race didn't stray much beyond the Big Three: Now it was down to Yale grad George W. Bush versus Harvard grad Al Gore. No Whittier or Eureka Colleges to spice up the action.

Trace said, "The only difficult thing about talking to him is that he still campaigns with every other sentence. He says George W. Bush is the sort of guy who was born on third base and thought he had hit a triple."

"Couldn't you say the same thing about Eric Beck?" Cliff asked.

"That's what I was thinking," Trace said. "But it turns out he's fed up with the whole trust fund game."

"How so?"

"He said he's had his parents' help for twenty-two years and he wants out. He figures the only way he's going to feel like his own man is to start afresh. He told me he wanted to give his money to charity, or maybe even to a political cause."

"Sounds very noble of young Eric," Cliff said.

Cliff had dealt with this phenomenon before. It was one of the reasons that intrafamily accounts could be so tricky. Wealthy parents had to decide how much money to give their children, and they didn't always agree. Which could lead to big-time squabbles. The Becks had divorced a few years before; if the split was money-related, it wouldn't be the first time. The irony of those situations was that the children didn't always want the money in the first place, for precisely the reasons Trace was describing. Generations with that mindset could be completely indifferent about what went on with their accounts.

"I don't suppose he was angry about URLybirds, then?" Cliff asked.

"Let's put it this way," Trace said. "I asked him if he was surprised that investors had given the company so much money without doing a thorough background check. He said no—that's what Republicans had done with George W. Bush."

Cliff wondered if Eric would take time off from his one-track mind just to kill Kyle Hooperman.

"You know, I still don't understand what this ticker-symbol thing is all about," Trace said.

"It could be the whole show," Cliff said. "The shot that killed Kyle Hooperman gave him a few seconds to live. Maybe he used that time to punch out his final ticker symbol—the initials of the person who killed him."

"You've been reading too many five-minute mysteries," Trace said.

"Yeah, maybe I have, but a man can dream, can't he? I just can't believe that Hooperman died with a TDL on his screen unless it meant something."

They were now on Route 495, better known as the Long Island Expressway. They took the LIE through Queens, then hooked a left onto the Cross Island Expressway for a few miles before getting off at Northern Boulevard. By New York standards, they had the roads to themselves.

"So I have a question," Trace said, a little dramatically.

"Yes?" Cliff asked. It was a long, high-pitched y-e-s, like Hardy used to give to Laurel.

"What was it exactly that made you leave Rutherford & Hayes?"

"Honestly?"

"Or you could lie through your teeth. Your choice."

"Honestly, what did it was a stock called Freddie Mac." Not a household name, according to Trace's blank stare.

"Freddie Mac is short for Federal Home Loan Mortgage Corporation," Cliff said.

Another blank stare.

"You see, Freddie Mac and Fannie Mae are the two government agencies that are responsible for creating a liquid market in home mortgages."

"What the hell does that mean?"

Cliff laughed. "You sound like a client," he said. "All you really need to know is that Freddie Mac buys mortgages and packages them as mortgage-backed securities. It's a cash machine. I bought the stock for a ton of clients in 1994 at about $60 per share. Thought it couldn't miss."

"But it did?"

"Not really. The stock is at $45 or so now, well off its highs, but there was a 4-for-1 split somewhere in between. So it's kept up with the market."

"Then what's the problem?"

"Well, what I didn't mention is that its first move was from $60 to $45," Cliff said. "At the low, my clients were 33 percent underwater."

"I repeat, what's the problem? It all worked out, didn't it?"

"Yeah, but they didn't know it then. I mean, I picked the absolute worst time to buy the stock. Interest rates were raised something like five times in 1994. Then the stock tanks, and clients ask me, 'Didn't you say that Freddie Mac can raise its earnings even if rates go up?' And I say 'Yes,' and then they ask me why the stock is going down. Others called up to tell me they discovered how leveraged the company is, and they want out. I try to tell them that the leverage is because Freddie Mac is a goddamn mortgage company, so its business is owning a lot of debt, and you shouldn't worry about it as long as the cost of the debt is lower than the return on the securities they package, which it was. They tell me it would be a lot easier not to worry if the stock was going up instead. Even the ones who considered themselves long-term investors had me on speed dial."

Cliff felt his temperature go up a little bit with the bad memory. The key word back in 1994 was "spread"—the difference between the rates paid out and the rates taken in. Freddie Mac and Fannie Mae weren't able to get their customary spreads that year, so they held back on their mortgage purchases rather than sacrifice long-term profitability. Not a bad move, but for the near term it meant that revenue growth was a trifle less than the market was expecting.

Some investors worried that spreads might be shrinking for good. The stock went down along with the entire financial sector.

A few hundred panicky phone calls later, at the beginning of the following year, spreads rebounded and so did Freddie Mac, Fannie Mae, Countrywide Credit, and practically any bank you could name. Dash Quillen called it the "potential energy" principle. In his view, when times are tough, quality stocks store their energy like a tightly wound spring. All it takes is for the worry to go away. The spring then bursts open to create kinetic energy. But sometimes you have to wait, that's all.

Cliff kept his thoughts to himself. He didn't feel like launching into an explanation of interest rate management and kinetic energy. That was the whole problem with Freddie Mac. Clients didn't really want to learn the intricacies of it, and Trace probably didn't either. Who could blame them? But Trace had a question of her own.

"Why did you buy Freddie Mac instead of Fannie Mae? Was it a guy thing?"

"I can't believe it," Cliff said. "You're still pissed because I don't think a woman killed Kyle Hooperman, aren't you?"

"Pissed? No. But I haven't forgotten our little side wager."

"I think I've spent it already," Cliff said.

Trace's question actually wasn't such a bad one. Cliff had thought he had bought Freddie Mac because it was smaller, and therefore had a greater opportunity for growth. But maybe there were factors behind his decision that he didn't even realize. The amusing part is that the choice hardly mattered: For most of the five years he had been following the stocks, they had moved in lockstep.

"Genders didn't matter," Cliff said. "What mattered was that I spent so much time consoling people about Freddie Mac that the whole thing didn't seem worth it. I sold the stock from some accounts because I couldn't stand it any more, and pretty soon I wasn't sure whether I wanted it to go up or down. When it finally did go up, some clients were happy, and the ones who sold called back to ask me why I didn't have the courage of my conviction. That's when I decided that if I was going to screw up, I'd do it for myself. If you can't be happy when you're up 300 percent, you can't be happy at all. That's my motto, and I'm sticking to it."

They had reached Sands Point in record time. No wonder it was considered such prime real estate. Maybe he could stop and get directions to Lenci's from Robin Leach. But directions weren't really necessary. Cliff had been to a party at Lenci's a few years back, when he and all the other R&H brokers were on the invitation list. Once you find Shore Road, you're almost home. Shore Road is the quintessentially ritzy address—Sands Point's answer to Park Avenue or even Rodeo Drive. It's a private road, full of speed bumps to discourage hoi polloi.

When Cliff and Trace reached Shore Road, there remained the small problem of remembering what the house looked like. Mansions can be maddeningly similar, especially at night. But they soon reached a spot where dozens of cars were parked along the side of the road. Had the Lencis asked their 100 best friends over for dinner and somehow forgotten to invite him this time? Had the guests from the prior party never left? Or had Lenci gotten the voice-mail message and arranged for all these cars to be here, just so the place would look the same?

Cliff and Trace got out and walked until they reached Lenci's driveway. It was recognizable after all, except that the first time around there hadn't been any TV vans on the premises. Nor had there been any bright lights from remote cameras. And there certainly hadn't been any yellow police tape spread around, but that's what stood between Cliff and any notion of approaching the front door.

About thirty feet away, a reporter with a Channel 5 microphone was telling her audience, live, that fund manager Dave Lenci had been shot.

CHAPTER 17

"Well, well, the famous shamus."

It was the identical greeting that Sean Cummings had used a few weeks before, but the little rodent was nowhere in sight. Instead, Cliff found himself face-to-face with Detective Jack Giardi, the pride of Westchester County and the point man for the Hooperman investigation. Perhaps Cummings would have been a better deal.

Jack Giardi seemed genetically engineered for police work. He had the relentlessness of a mongoose forged on a body that was stocky enough to call balls and strikes in the big leagues. To top things off, he had this deep, gravelly voice that was terrible for karaoke but great when it came to intimidating poor civilians.

"To what do I owe this honor, Cavanaugh?" Giardi asked.

"The honor is all mine. A bit off your beat, aren't you, Jack?" Sands Point and Rye were only a few miles apart as the crow flies, but crows don't usually fly across Long Island Sound.

Giardi said, "When two guys from the same firm start catching bullets, even Sands Point's finest can use a little backup. What's your excuse?"

"I just wanted to pitch an umbrella at Jones Beach before the summer crowd moved in. Must have taken a wrong turn, I guess." Cliff flashed the same smile that had worked so well with Maude the barmaid. Giardi wasn't quite as smitten.

"Look, we got things well under control, Cavanaugh, so how about you put your roadster in reverse? Maybe you'll make it back to the city before your chickie's bedtime." Giardi had positioned himself alongside the yellow police tape, as if to remind Cliff and Trace that whatever the actual jurisdiction was on the Lenci shooting, he was still inside to their outside.

In Cliff's brief experience with homicide investigations, local authorities were about as helpful as galoshes in the Everglades. So there was no surprise here. But he wasn't in the mood to be drawn into any pillow fights, at least not with someone who was carrying a much bigger pillow. Chivalry wasn't dead. It was just playing possum.

Behind Giardi, camera lights were going on and off as the media took turns with their thirty-second spiels. They were all saying the same thing. Lenci had been shot sometime earlier that evening and had been taken to North Shore Hospital. Condition unknown. Also unknown was whether he had caught a glimpse of his assailant.

"Can I assume it's too early to link this case to the Hooperman murder?" Cliff asked.

"Ballistics is gathering data even as we speak, oh famous one."

He'd said *dah*-ta, not *day*-ta, a surefire way to get under Cliff's skin. That and the toothpick Giardi kept moving from one side of his mouth to the other, like a crazed metronome.

"Well, as long as we're waiting, do you happen to have any leads on the Hooperman case?" Cliff asked.

"If I did, I wouldn't be sharing them with you, now, would I?"

"Better watch out, Jack," Cliff said. "A few more quips like that and I'll drop you from my AOL buddy list."

Trace said, "He's just jealous, Cliff. I doubt they've investigated things as thoroughly as you have."

Cliff hoped Trace would notice that he had stopped breathing, but no such luck.

"I bet they've never even heard of Eric Beck," she said.

"Eric Beck! The ultimate mama's boy? Is that who we're talking about here?" Giardi let out a crusty laugh that was two-thirds Marlboro and one-third Miller High Life.

Cliff looked at Trace for a second, recalling that she had cast Eric Beck as a modern-day Abbie Hoffman. Men and women were supposed to see things differently, but this was ridiculous.

"Aw, come on," Giardi said. "Even a junior sleuth like you should know that young Eric took his mother out to dinner the night Hooperman was killed. A little birthday celebration at the Four Seasons, no less. Loin of venison for him, Colorado lamb chops for her. Want me to tell you what they had for dessert?"

"I hear the Four Seasons makes a wonderful alibi soufflé," Cliff said.

Trace had decided by now that the best defense was a good offense. She said, "Fine, you know the details on Eric Beck, we know the details on Milton Koenig. It'll all come out in the wash."

"Milton Koenig? The musician? Is that where you've been spending your time? Milton Koenig?" Giardi stepped away from the yellow police tape. "This is too rich, Cavanaugh. I take back what I said about hitting the road. You and your little chickie here are making my night."

"Happy to oblige," Cliff said.

"Hey, Cavanaugh, I've got an idea," Giardi said. "Why don't you check out someone like Jeremy Nash instead of wasting your time on people who never threatened Hooperman's life?"

"Nash couldn't have done it," Trace said. "He was on eBay when Hooperman was killed."

Giardi started shaking his head. "Sorry to disappoint you, sweetie, but we looked into that, too. According to eBay records, the Springstine tickets were sold at 5:00 P.M., which I don't need to remind you was several hours before Hooperman was killed."

"That's Springsteen," Cliff said. "The Boss."

"You can call him anything you want," Giardi said. "Whatever makes you happy."

Cliff was anything but happy. Not if "Brash Nash" had pulled one over on him.

"But as long as we're talking about analysts at dear old Rutherford & Hayes, you really should watch your old friend Lou Battaglia a bit more closely. He didn't like Hooperman any more than Nash did."

"Jack, if you're up on things as much as you say you are, you know that Lou was on *Moneyline* that night," Cliff said.

"Yeah, that's right, and do you happen to know where *Moneyline* is shot from?" Giardi asked.

Cliff again went short of breath. He saw immediately what Giardi was driving at. The CNN studios are on Eighth Avenue, between 33rd and 34th Streets, practically next door to the Post Office. More to the point, all of half a block from Penn Station. If Lou had wanted to dispatch of Hooperman, he could have hopped on an Amtrak train to Rye, walked to Oneida Road, pulled out his concealed handgun, and then walked back to pick up a local train to Grand Central. At least, that's what Giardi seemed to be implying.

"I didn't realize you were prone to fantasies, Jack."

Cliff couldn't help but have a fantasy of his own. Surely *Moneyline* wouldn't have let an ashen character like Lou Battaglia on their show without sprucing him up a bit. Cliff wondered if the homicide guys poring over Hooperman's body had found any traces of stage makeup.

Giardi said, "Well, if you're so sure your friends didn't do it, why don't you tell me what *you* were doing that night, Cavanaugh?"

"Huh?"

"Tsk, tsk," Giardi said. "You didn't think we'd erase your voice-mail message, did you?"

"Hey, I can explain that," Cliff said.

"No need," Giardi said. "But that's your car down there on the left, isn't it?"

"What about my car?"

"Well, it just so happens that a car very much like this one was spotted in Hooperman's neighborhood the night he was killed. Thought you'd like to know." Giardi was smiling wide enough for Cliff to see the gold caps on his ten-year molars.

Trace took another look at Cliff's wheels and noticed something that she hadn't paid attention to the first time around. It was the finest Swedish engineering, all right. A bright, shiny, black Saab Turbo.

■ ■ ■

"Well, that was the most embarrassing evening of my life."

Cliff was once again behind the wheel, this time headed back to Manhattan. He didn't even bother to stop by at North Shore Hospital, mostly out of fear that Giardi might follow them there. Whatever happened to Lenci was going to happen, and they'd find out about it soon enough. A light rain had started at about eleven o'clock, but Long Island wasn't feeling puddle-wonderful in the least.

"It wasn't so bad, Cliffie."

"Not so bad? That's what you call me being humiliated by a fat-assed toothpick chewer? Not so bad?" Cliff was gripping the steering wheel like it was a chin-up bar.

"At least we picked up some pieces of information we didn't have before," Trace said. Part of her job was to find silver linings from Brillo pads, but in this case the boss wasn't buying.

Cliff said, "Yeah, but only because fat-ass had beaten us to the punch. He did everything but tell me what I had for dinner the night Hooperman was killed."

"Well, what did you have?"

"I can't remember," Cliff said. "I was hoping Jack could tell me. If I liked it, I'd have it again."

"Do you think he knew that Lucky Sparks drives a car that looks just like this one?" Trace asked.

"It really does?" Cliff asked.

" 'Fraid so," Trace said. "If they're not twins, they're at least fellow octuplets."

"I doubt Giardi knew a damn thing," Cliff said. "Just because a car was spotted in the neighborhood doesn't mean anything. Some lost squash player could have been trying to find the Apawamis Club."

"The Kiwanis Club?"

"That's Apawamis. It's an old-line country club that happens to be located two blocks from Hooperman's house."

"Does Lucky Sparks play golf there?"

"Not at night he doesn't, and probably not back in February, either," Cliff said. "Don't you see how full of crap Giardi was? He tossed out all those scenarios, trying to make us suspicious of four people at the same time, when the truth is that, at most, one of these scenarios was real. We have no idea what kind of car the killer drove, if any. Besides, we're talking about Westchester County. Saying the killer drove a Saab is like narrowing down the Stockholm Strangler to someone named Johannesen."

"So what's your take on the TDL symbol now?" Trace asked.

"Well, if my brain would just function like a human being's, which I guess it's decided not to do, then I'd be thinking along different lines than I was on the way out here."

"Such as?"

"Such as the fact that the killer could have left the TDL up there, maybe as a private little joke saying, 'Here's my next victim. Try and stop me.' "

"But why Hooperman and Lenci?"

"Couldn't tell you," Cliff said. "But I can tell you that Hannah Diehl specifically told me that Lenci handled the IPO game just the way Hooperman did. If so, he gives Shari Beck special treatment and someone else isn't too happy about it."

"Hoop gave Shari special treatment? Is that in my notes somewhere?"

"It's in my mental construct," Cliff said. "My guess is that the entire URLybirds disaster started because Shari wanted shares and then changed her mind when she saw what a lemon it was."

"You can do that?"

"You shouldn't be able to, no; but in the real world it could happen, assuming Hooperman acted quickly enough. He could have done an ex post facto switcheroo and allotted her shares to some of his poor, unsuspecting other clients."

"Seems like a lot of trouble," Trace said.

"No question," Cliff said. "But maybe he didn't want to take another hit on his error account and get Sean Cummings on his case. We already saw that Milton Koenig didn't know about the shares in advance, which is a real no-no. A portfolio manager is supposed to get permission from his clients when it comes to IPOs, even for discretionary accounts. So something's wrong. I just don't know how much."

"Let me amend that," Cliff added. "I don't know much at all."

Several minutes went by without conversation. Cliff was hungry, but not much was open along the way. Licking one's own wounds wasn't particularly nutritious, but it would have to do.

Finally, Trace said, "I think I've got just the ticket for what ails you."

"What's that?"

"Tell me something really, really embarrassing."

"That's supposed to work?"

"Emotions don't mind being manipulated. We do it back at Stella Adler all the time. If I can't cry on cue, I'll pull out a nose hair or two."

"I thought Olivier said you didn't have to resort to tricks like that."

"What he meant was that Olivier didn't have to. C'mon, Cliff. It'll get your mind off Giardi, I promise you."

Cliff's first thoughts involved some bogus stocks he had bought over the years. He had bought Advanced Micro Devices a few years before, eschewing industry leader Intel and violating one of Dash Quillen's maxims in the process. Dash used to preach, "You don't have to be original to win at this game," which was basically a warning not to get too clever for your own good. Or not to bet on the underdog unless the market gives you preposterous odds. Which it didn't in this case. Advanced Micro did a seesaw act for four years while Intel acted like a true Silicon Valley blue chip and went higher and higher. That was embarrassing. Ever since then, Cliff resolved that if he was ever going to take a flier on a company that was number two in its industry, he should at least buy shares of the leader as a hedge.

But it was clear that Trace wasn't interested in hearing another market tale, even one of woe. All Cliff could think of was the fact that the Carpenters' Christmas song made him cry. But that was nobody's business. And coming clean certainly wasn't going to make him feel any better. He thought some more.

"Got it," Cliff said, after a twenty-second pause.

"Really embarrassing?"

"Utterly and truly," Cliff said. "But I'll let you be the judge."

"I'm all ears."

"It was the first time I took a date to an expensive restaurant," Cliff said. "Belinda Vanderpeel was her name. Real sophisticated type, a world traveler. I think she was Miss Teenage Luxembourg or something like that." Trace shifted in her seat and turned down the radio a tad. It was now playing an old Leo Sayer tune, so there was no harm done.

"The waiter asked me if I wanted to order wine with dinner. I said yes, even though I didn't really drink the stuff. I saw Belinda out of the corner of my eye. She looked like she was just waiting to be impressed. So when the waiter offered me the wine list I just waved it off. I said, 'No need, let's just make it a nice Chateaubriand for two.' "

Cliff stopped for a moment and the only sound was a muted but still squeaky-pitched Leo Sayer, like he was trying to escape from the dashboard.

Cliff shook his head. All of a sudden he grinned at Trace. "Okay, you win. Giardi was nothing compared to that."

CHAPTER 18

By the next day, Trace's efforts at mood therapy for Cliff had lapsed into history. Saturday morning was the sort of morning where you wake up and think for a second that everything is okay, and suddenly you remember what happened the day before and you realize that the world is a miserable place. That was the view from Cliff Cavanaugh's personal crow's nest on March 18, 2000.

Life was unfair. Why did his parents insist that he say *day*-ta, not *dah*-ta, if it wasn't going to do him any good? It would be one thing if a great big palooka had made physical mincemeat of him, but this was mental mincemeat, and it hurt even worse.

As Cliff gave the night some thought, he realized that at least one of Jack Giardi's scenarios contained a giant bluff. Even if Giardi knew that Lucky Sparks drove a Saab, there was no chance that his car was connected to Hooperman's murder. Sparks had bought the car with the proceeds from URLybirds, which he sold just two days before Hooperman's murder. No way he could have gotten the money in time. The sale of stock involves a trade date and a settlement date. The seller doesn't get the money until all the paperwork is done and the trade can settle, which usually takes three business days.

It used to take five. Not only that; back in the early '80s, if you wanted to sell a stock to take a loss for tax purposes, you couldn't wait until December 31, because the tax date was considered the settlement date, and the trade wouldn't settle until early in the new year. The rule was changed to make the trade date the tax date, but that didn't change the fundamental fact that trades don't settle immediately. You don't get your money until day T + 3.

Besides, Lucky Sparks just didn't seem like the murdering type. If he really did kill Hooperman, he'd go to jail; if he went to jail, he'd fall behind on his Wee Burn dues; and if he fell behind on his Wee Burn dues, his name would be posted on the club bulletin board for all his fellow members to see. No way he'd allow that.

And what about Jeremy Nash? So what if eBay records showed that his ticket purchase had been made at 5:00 P.M.? The company was based in San Jose. Wasn't it possible that they kept their records in Pacific Time? Could Giardi really be that dumb? A man can dream, can't he?

Cliff's first move was to go to the homepage of DeathNet, the leading online obituary service. DeathNet lets you create your own personal Watchlists, and the service will alert you via e-mail if anybody on your list should unexpectedly depart. Donald Trump was a particularly popular request. Alternatively, DeathNet lets you enter a name, date, and ZIP code, whereupon the system will search for matches.

It turned out that only a handful of people whose last names began with "L" had died in the Long Island area in the past 24 hours, and Dave Lenci wasn't among them. But just in case things went the wrong way, Cliff put Lenci on his Watchlist. He declined Death-Net's trademarked FloraFirst option, which would have automatically sent a bouquet of lilies to the deceased's relatives.

Cliff wondered idly whether Mario Gabelli would have made use of DeathNet if the service had been available earlier. Back in the '80s, when Gabelli was a regular on those annual roundtables at *Barron's*, he seemed to know the exact ages of all the dottering CEOs in his portfolio. The investment premise was that when a majority shareholder passed away, a company could become ripe for takeover. Earl Scheib, the auto painting company named after its raspy-voiced founder, was one of Gabelli's perennial favorites. When Scheib died in 1995, shares of his company popped 2 points, from 4 to 6, just as Gabelli had foreseen. A fifty percent overnight gain is nothing to sneeze at—unless you had invested eight years earlier and watched it go from 15 down to 4. The other flaw in the strategy was that no takeover ever appeared. The company was squeezed by higher raw materials costs and consumer resistance to higher paint job prices, and the stock slumped to just $2 a share by 1999. Even a statistically cheap stock doesn't make for a good takeover candidate if its business is in secular decline, unless you're confident that would-be suitors won't figure that out.

Cliff went to a newsstand near Columbus Circle to see how the tabloids were handling the Lenci shooting. The story, like West Coast night games, didn't make the *Times,* but the *Daily News* headline writers came up with "Double Trouble," which seemed as good a description as any. The *Post* opted for "The St. Patrick's Day Massacre," which was something of an exaggeration. Then again, "famous shamus" felt like a whopping exaggeration relative to the current state of Cliff's biorhythms. Now it was more like "dumbshit gumshoe," which wasn't quite as mellifluous but had the benefit of up-to-the-minute accuracy.

Fortunately, the papers *did* agree on the basic facts of the case. Lenci, like Kyle Hooperman before him, had been shot once from close range. Except this time the shot was all of an inch and a half to the right. It had missed Lenci's heart, but it nicked an artery as it tore through the side of his chest. If he hadn't been found promptly, he would have been DeathNet material for sure.

The person doing the finding was Lenci's wife Suzanne. She had just dropped off their son and daughter at friends' houses, a sort of suburban quid pro quo for the circus venture. Upon returning home, her headlights caught her husband in the middle of their semicircular driveway, the same driveway Cliff saw on Friday night between glimpses of Jack Giardi's gold caps. She called an ambulance immediately. She remained by her husband's side in the ambulance, which explained to Cliff why he had seen two cars in the driveway. One was a Ford Suburban, and behind it was a silver Jaguar.

Big deal.

■ ■ ■

Trace's day was the biorhythmic equivalent of Cliff's. The bottom line of the prior evening's fiasco was that she was being outperformed by an Internet database. The only way to make amends was to do something the database could not.

Her mission had actually begun the previous night. After Cliff dropped her off at Washington Square, she hooked up with a Tisch music school student who was nursing his seventh green beer. Trace persuaded him that he should avoid loud noises for at least twenty-four hours. Loud noises like the clashing of cymbals or even the plaintive wail of a contrabassoon. Appreciative of her concern for his welfare, he yielded his ticket for the New York Philharmonic.

Redemption was at stake, and eight o'clock could not come soon enough. Trace spent much of the day memorizing lines she had already memorized—not such a great strategy. Once you've got the lines down, you're supposed to work on things like voice modulation, eye contact, and all those other details that separate Helen Hayes from Tori Spelling. But Trace's heart wasn't in it. She was so out of it, she was early. It wasn't even 7:30 when she got to the Astor Place subway entrance, a little gazebo that looked like a nineteenth-century sculpture. She took the uptown Lex to Grand Central, shuttled to the West Side, connected with a northbound #1 train, and, minutes later, was at Columbus Circle, a short walk from Lincoln Center.

As she walked along, she was passed by a couple of power walkers in dark sweats, with yellow reflective strips wrapped around their arms. She thought of Cliff, for no particular reason. Maybe it was because he wouldn't power walk under any circumstance. She got out her cell phone and started to give him a call, but hung up at the first ring. There was no need to advertise her intentions that evening. If anything good came from her efforts, she could always tell him later. For now, it was on to Lincoln Center's Avery Fisher Hall.

The Lincoln Center for the Performing Arts is one of Manhattan's prized possessions. Its profile is an open rectangular frame with an array of six-story pillars. A fountain in front is surrounded by a stone plaza. When you step inside Avery Fisher Hall, you immediately have the feel of 1950s architecture, with wood paneling and orange seats. Hanging from the walls and ceiling are various arch shapes that were added more recently, no doubt on the recommendation of some high-priced acoustics consultant.

Trace approached her seat uneasily. For all the time she had spent in theaters, she wasn't particularly savvy when it came to the New York Philharmonic or to orchestral performances in general. The headliners for the evening were not what you'd call household names. The featured performer was pianist Leif Ove Andsnes. The conductor was someone named Valery Gergiev, who looked not altogether unlike a young John Belushi. But it was Trace's good fortune that the Philharmonic had only one contrabassoonist, so Milton Koenig figured to be an easy mark.

Trace took her opera glasses out of her pocketbook and gazed to where the woodwinds seemed to be congregated. All she knew about a contrabassoon is that it was bigger than an ordinary bassoon. Of course, ordinary bassoons weren't exactly piccolo-sized, and there seemed to be quite a few of them. But upon closer inspection, one of them stood out as the queen bee. Behind it was a distinguished looking gentleman with a grayish-white goatee and gold wire-rimmed glasses. Trace tried kidding herself that she could distinguish his notes from the rest of the woodwinds. Which was as good a way as any to pass the time, because there remained the matter of waiting out the remainder of the concert. The program was slated to begin with "Poem of Ecstasy," by someone named Scriabin. After that, the composers got more familiar. Piano Concerto No. 3 by Prokofiev was followed by Beethoven's Symphony No. 6, the Pastoral. Trace suddenly realized that she could have arrived at intermission and still have accomplished her goal. Sitting for three hours wasn't exactly her style. But no matter. By any reckoning, there were worse ways to spend an evening.

■ ■ ■

Back at the home office, Cliff checked DeathNet for about the eighth time. Still no sign of Lenci. But as long as Cliff was online, he wanted to check on a feeling that had been nagging him ever since Trace's most recent e-mail, which by now wasn't even all that recent. He went to altavista.digital.com and typed in "This Is Not Your Father's Stockpicking Book."

Ten Web pages turned up. There were a couple of reviews and a couple of bookstore listings, none of which had anything interesting to say. Near the end of the list was an entry called "Talking Books topics." That was more like it. Perhaps Milton Koenig really *was* listening to an audio version of the book, even though the traditional sources denied its existence.

Alas, the "Talking Books topics" Web page was about as helpful as an intercom in a hearse. The page was nothing but a listing of book/audio titles that had been added to a particular library in 1997. The titles didn't have much in common: "Monsters of the Sea," "Murderers and Other Friends," "Letters of Robert Louis Stevenson," and about 50 others. "This Is Not Your Father's Stockpicking Book" was two-thirds of the way down on the list. The URL for the Web page was www.loc.gov/nls/tbt/1997-6-tbtmf.html, which was all well and good except that everything in between the www and the html might as well have been Serbo-Croatian. Cliff clicked on the URL and began deleting from the right until he came up with www.loc.gov/nls, presumably the parent page. Now it looked more intelligible. The loc.gov part looked like local government. And if it was a government listing about books, the nls part probably stood for National Library Service. Cliff hit the return key and waited for the new page to appear. Using a Stone Age computer was costly at times like this, but as long as his waiting time was measured in seconds, not minutes, Cliff was willing to live with it. He convinced himself that he enjoyed seeing images formed one pixel at a time. Finally, the new page materialized.

Cliff said, "Omigod."

■ ■ ■

When the concert was over, Trace took her sore butt to the musicians' entrance on 65th Street. There was something creepy about asking where the musicians came and went from, something positively Hinckleyesque. But Trace meant no harm, assuming that a couple of minutes with Milton Koenig wouldn't be harmful. From the number of musicians who kept piling out, the New York Philharmonic had twice the roster of the New York Giants. All she wanted was a glimpse of that grayish-white goatee. It would be a shame to miss him after all this effort. But missing Koenig turned out to be the least of Trace's worries. Suddenly there he was, all of twelve feet away. And he was carrying more than a contrabassoon. Trace said. "Omigod."

The extra item he was carrying was a white cane.

She quickly grabbed her cell phone from her pocketbook, the same cell phone she had turned in to Avery Fisher Hall security for the duration of the concert. What a good doobie she was. She hit the redial button, hoping that the security personnel hadn't called Madagascar during the Prokofiev piece. She braced herself to give Cliff some bad news. And she kicked herself for agreeing to an employment contract that didn't include severance pay.

"Cliff, I have to make a confession. I missed a detail about Milton Koenig that you just might consider important."

"You mean the fact that he's blind?" Cliff said.

"You know? How could you know?"

"I found out about thirty minutes ago. You remember the book he was listening to, the one I claimed had never come out on audio?"

"Yeah," Trace said. She watched limp-eyed as Milton Koenig climbed into the back of one of the waiting limos.

"Well, it only came out on a special format that the National Library Service makes as a service to the blind. If you tried it on a normal tape player, it wouldn't work."

"I guess it wouldn't help to say that he didn't seem blind over the phone," she said.

"Trace, you did your job. If I hadn't been so slow, we would have ruled him out ages ago."

"Are you serious?"

"Completely serious. And you helped me rule out Lucky Sparks as well. We're making progress."

"We are? I mean, I did?"

Trace was grateful that Cliff didn't seem particularly angry about another sin of omission. She figured he was pleased with himself for once again using financial information to its fullest advantage. Maybe there was something to the idea of investing, then investigating.

But the truth was that Cliff was too stunned to be angry. All he could see was Jack Giardi's shiteating grin.

CHAPTER 19

When the new workweek began, Rutherford & Hayes was quaking in its boots. The place had managed to take Hooperman's murder in stride, but a murder attempt on top of that was pushing people over the edge. Investments were no longer the most important force of the day. Intel and Cisco were hitting new highs, yet it was no match for Sean Cummings's blood pressure.

As for Dave Lenci, the picture was improving. He had been removed from the critical list and was resting comfortably. A hospital spokesperson suggested that he would be able to go home soon. At least, that's what the Monday morning papers said. Cliff figured he should at least know what everyone else knew. But if he truly wanted to keep his competitive edge, a field trip to Sands Point was in order.

Unfortunately, the North Shore Hospital parking lot was no way to spend an afternoon.

Cliff had brought along all the stakeout essentials he could think of: his complete set of Lynyrd Skynyrd tapes, two cans of Jolt cola, a couple of Drake's coffee cakes, and, last but not least, a copy of Vincent Di Maio's classic, *Gunshot Wounds: Practical Aspects of Firearms, Ballistics, and Forensic Techniques*. Di Maio was the chief medical examiner in Bexar County, Texas. Reading his book was a little like reading *National Geographic*, where they sucker you with a dozen pages of panda bears and then nail you with a grinning fruit bat. Only this time the photos all came from the resident shutterbug at the San Antonio morgue. Bonnie and Clyde got off easy compared to some of these poor clowns, none of whom had the opportunity to sign photo release forms.

Ninety minutes had passed without a sign of Suzanne Lenci. Cliff hoped this wasn't how Sergeant Joe Friday and Officer Bill Gannon spent the day watch out of bunco division. The good news was that, barring an untimely lapse, the prey was going to show up. Cliff had managed to park himself five spaces away from the same Ford Suburban he had seen in Lenci's driveway. When your license plate reads MUNNEY, it's hard to travel incognito.

Somewhere during the 123rd minute of Cliff's vigil, a woman with an unmistakable bounce to her walk emerged from the hospital's double doors. Cliff set forth from his bunker and moved toward the hospital at a heavy-hearted pace until the mark was within striking distance.

The woman was wearing an olive trenchcoat and had a bright red earwarmer circling her forehead, pushing up a nest of thick, brown hair. Between the earwarmer and a pair of round, tortoise-shell sunglasses, she had enough of her face covered to satisfy the Ayatollah. But she was who she was, all right. In the world of trophy wives, Suzanne Lenci was the Heisman and the Conn Smythe, all wrapped into one five-foot, six-inch brunette package.

Stories surrounding the Lencis and their marriage had been circulating for years. Everyone knew about his long hours, and no one thought she spent her idle time knitting and purling. The stories reached a peak at the time of the famous summer party on Shore Road, when she wore a Danskin Emma Peel outfit and came on to the entire institutional sales department. It was just a tease, but it didn't go unnoticed. Throughout the next week, otherwise mild-mannered investment bankers were seen punching their fists into their bulletin boards. Underwriting initiatives came to a standstill. If Goldman Sachs had been smart, they'd have sponsored another party the following year. But Dave Lenci had seen enough. He put his partner in moth-balls, and if anyone had seen her since, they weren't talking.

Cliff had a bona fide sighting at about ten paces. He stopped and hoped he remained recognizable.

He cleared his throat and said, "Excuse me."

"Oh, hi," Suzanne Lenci said, as she quickly cocked her head to the side. She didn't mention any names, but Cliff felt a step up from total anonymity.

He stretched out his right hand. "Cliff Cavanaugh. I'm a former colleague of your husband's. I was just hoping he was doing all right."

She took his hand with both of her own, like he was helping her stand up. "I thought you looked familiar. You're nice to ask. He's doing much better, thanks."

She let go after a moment or two. She took off her sunglasses and placed them in her coat pocket. Cliff looked up at the murky gray sky and realized that she didn't really need them. Sunglasses were just something women wore when faced with an emotionally distressing situation. Except that Suzanne's mascara was as unsullied as Trent Lott's hair. Maybe the shades were to cover up the fact that she *wasn't* crying.

"I'm glad to hear he's okay," Cliff said. "The whole office is in shock."

Suzanne Lenci sighed. "I'm just relieved that the children didn't have to see what I saw."

"I understand," Cliff said. Even assuming that the Lencis had called off their conjugal visits, the scene couldn't have been a pleasant one. Husband lying lifelessly, a pool of blood on the driveway, plus the fear that a killer might still be lurking.

"If he hadn't insisted on going back to work after the show was over, none of this would have happened," she said.

"He's got a demanding job, no question about that," Cliff said. He noted to himself that if Lenci would rather cozy up with the GE annual report than with Suzanne, he was brain dead, no matter what the hospital was saying.

"What really gives me the creeps is that someone must have been following our every move," she said. "Living on a private road used to make me feel safe, but now it seems so dark and lonely. Do you know what I mean, Mr. Cavanaugh?"

Cliff's eyes widened. Had he heard what he thought he heard? Nah. It didn't seem possible. This was a woman who had come within three-quarters of an inch of becoming a widow. Then again, this was a community where the widow was the one in the black tennis dress. *The black widow.* That's what the institutional sales force called her to this day. Maybe all the stories about her were true after all. For someone who had been out of practice for two years, she was doing awfully well. It was time to stay focused.

Cliff asked, "So who could have known that you were coming back from the circus?"

"That's what so eerie," she said, shaking her head. "We had been talking about going for a couple of weeks, but Dave wasn't able to get his plans together until the evening before we actually went. I'm sure he told his staff at work and maybe a few clients, but that's it."

His staff. Oh, brother, Cliff thought. Only if Hannah Diehl developed a multiple personality disorder.

Cliff asked, "So was there anything troubling him in the days before the shooting? Did he seem agitated or distracted or anything like that?"

"Well, I suppose he may have been a bit agitated recently, but that's how he gets sometimes in volatile markets. It wasn't unusual."

"Would you say he was depressed?"

"What a curious question, Mr. Cavanaugh."

"I'm a curious guy," Cliff said. "That's what people tell me, anyway. They say, 'Cliff Cavanaugh, you're sure a curious guy.' "

Suzanne Lenci smiled. "So you are," she said. "But this was an attempted homicide, not an attempted suicide. They didn't find a gun, you know."

"So I've heard," Cliff said.

"Say, now I know where I've heard your name," she said, sticking out a nicely manicured index finger. "You left a message on our voice mail the night Dave was shot, didn't you?"

"Who, me?" Cliff said.

"Yes, you. Didn't you say you were coming over that night? Detective Giardi told me to watch out for you. He said you were a suspect."

"Yeah, right. And I've come to finish the job, only I've gone out of my way to chat up the missus beforehand." Cliff reached into his wallet and pulled out one of his Moribund Stanley business cards. It was as close as he could get to showing her his badge.

Suzanne Lenci scanned the card and she seemed a trifle embarrassed. She absentmindedly brushed her hair with her right hand. "So I don't have to frisk you, is that what you're telling me?"

Gulp.

Not only was she talking about frisking, she had given "the signal." That's what Cliff's old friend Oscar Bonaventure called it. Oscar taught it to Cliff in his early years as an eligible bachelor: When a woman looks at you and touches her hair, she's attracted to you, period. It's not like some stock market indicator that only works 40 percent of the time. This one was 100 percent, barring head lice.

Cliff tried to tell himself that his imagination was playing tricks on him. Surely she had no intention of bringing him back home to Shore Road, back to her live-in help and two screaming kids. Then he thought of the Ford Suburban. The tinted windows. Is that what she had in mind? Couldn't she at least wait until he'd made out his will?

Time to start talking about the husband again.

Cliff said, "Well, it won't be long before Dave comes home, I don't imagine."

"He's coming home tomorrow," she said. "But you know Dave. The market never rests. I'm sure he'll be back in his office by Thursday morning."

"Did he happen to get a look at whoever shot him?"

"I'm afraid not. It was dark. Whoever it was must have sneaked up on him."

Cliff remembered the scene on Shore Road that Friday night. The pool of Lenci's blood was located right near the front steps. Someone could have been hiding behind one of the two topiary ducks in front. Probably the one to the left of the house. Whoever it was could have gotten plenty close. And must have, judging by the powder marks on Lenci's suit. It occurred to Cliff that Lenci wore Brooks Brothers suits. It was one of history's great enigmas that all four assassinated U.S. presidents were shot while wearing Brooks Brothers suits. Coincidence, or just high market share?

There were more questions where that one came from. Did Suzanne return immediately after the shooting? Was the killer behind the duck when she arrived? If so, did he leave any footprints?

"Well, I really have to get in and talk with him. I'm sure he'll have a lot to say."

"As you wish, Mr. Cavanaugh," she said, and turned toward her car. She had only gone about six feet when Cliff spoke up.

"Say, do you mind if I ask you a question?"

Suzanne turned around and shook her head back and forth a couple of times. More of a wriggle than a shake, actually.

"You usually drive a Ford Suburban, right?"

"That's right," she said. "It's right over there, as a matter of fact." Cliff had to remember to at least show some curiosity about the direction she was pointing in.

"So it is," Cliff said.

"Why do you ask? Do you like cars, Mr. Cavanaugh?"

"I do, as a matter of fact," Cliff said. "But I was just thinking. The night your husband was shot, did you back into the driveway?"

"Another one of your curious questions, Cliff Cavanaugh. Just what makes you ask that?"

"I read the papers," Cliff said. "I saw a picture in the *Post* and noticed that the Jaguar was parked behind the Suburban. It seemed odd to me, that's all."

"Well, I don't mean to disappoint you, but Dave just thought it would be a lot of fun for the kids to ride in his Jaguar. They rarely got the chance, and they loved it almost as much as he did."

"So he took the Suburban as part of the whole circus treat he had prepared?"

"Exactly," she said. "He took it into town that morning and drove it back that night. He went to the office when the circus was over, just so he could return his calls before the end of the week. Clients come first, you know."

Cliff said, "Oh, I know. Dave has done more for his clients than most people realize."

He let it go at that, and started walking toward the hospital. Except that now he was the one who only went six feet.

"Oh, Mister Cavanaugh, one more thing."

"What's that?"

"Dave is taking a nap. Visiting hours are over."

CHAPTER 20

If Monday had its frustrating moments, Tuesday had the potential to be even worse. Most self-respecting sleuths would avoid a room full of red herrings. But Cliff pressed on.

The room was Salon Beaumont at the Meridien Hotel, where Rutherford & Hayes was sponsoring a luncheon on behalf of Gumbegone and its initial public offering. A few such salons were tucked behind the first-floor elevator bank, and they were all the same: an innocuous blend of beige wallpaper, burgundy-colored draperies, and dark stained wood trim. The inhabitants were the usual suspects: white-shirted institutional portfolio managers. And there was a red herring at every place setting.

That was to be expected. "Red herring" was the trade name for a preliminary prospectus, so-called because of the red ink at the top, specifically warning that the prospectus was preliminary to the actual offering. The red herring had all the financial information you could ever want, together with paragraphs covering topics such as the company's intended use of the proceeds, and special risk factors. One of the risk factors amused Cliff: There was no existing public market for the shares, which of course was the whole point of the luncheon and others like it on the Gumbegone road show. The collective input of everyone who came to see the company would be reflected in the stock's offering price, and possibly in the number of shares that would ultimately be sold.

Investors use many different strategies at luncheons such as this one. Some park themselves down at the head table and make the CEO give more answers than Alex Trebek. Others seek out the chief financial officer instead, on the grounds that the CFO isn't necessarily surrounded by brokerage house muckety-mucks, so you can get greater candor that way. Both strategies work surprisingly often, because the prime seats can remain as unclaimed as the last chocolate eclair at an Amy Vanderbilt dinner party. Just because everyone wants it doesn't mean anyone touches it.

Cliff had never been bashful about where to position himself. Over the years, he had sat next to such luminaries as Jack Welch of GE, Jim Clark of Netscape, and Jeff Bezos of Amazon. For this particular luncheon, only one place setting had any interest: the one next to Constantine Dimitriades.

Constantine Dimitriades was in his mid-fifties but was eternally swarthy. He had the snub nose of a middleweight boxer, a slight space between his two front teeth, and a EEE-width face with as many bumps and dimples as a Hubbard squash. He was a gregarious sort, full of pomp, circumstance, and opinions. All of which meant that he wasn't particularly hard to spot, and as soon as the dinner bell sounded, Cliff shadowed him all the way to the corner table.

For all of Dimitriades's vitality, Cliff felt a bit awkward sitting next to him. Knowing that someone is about to lose his job is like knowing that someone's wife is cheating on him. Cliff was the man who knew too much. This was not the time to be talking about Leslie Peterborough, golden parachutes, or the wonderful job-search capabilities of Monster.com.

But if Dimitriades was on the endangered species list, he sure as hell didn't show it. He confidently forecast to the table that the Dow would hit 20,000 within two years, and it was apparent that he fully intended to be along for the ride. Someone pointed out that if Microsoft and Intel had replaced Goodyear and Sears in 1995 rather than in 1999, the Dow might already be pushing 20,000. Dimitriades seemed amused at the arbitrariness of it all. He made the observation that the Dow Jones committee was the saddest bunch of investors he had ever seen. They never added a stock until it had racked up at least a decade of outstanding growth. Then someone across the table spoiled the fun by asking: If the Dow was such a rearview-mirror portfolio, how did it keep going up? Fred Gletz would have been proud.

Dimitriades switched the subject. He pointed to the table next to theirs, where an analyst was on his cell phone, trying to look important. That was all Dimitriades needed for a segue into how he had held on to Motorola through thick and thin and come out a hero. Cliff looked to Dimitriades's left and saw a junior portfolio manager type, a young bunny rabbit with a size-16 shirt on a size-14 neck. He was hanging on every word.

If it had been 1998 instead, Cliff felt pretty sure that Motorola would never have entered the conversation. Back then, the company seemed to disappoint investors with every quarterly earnings report. The stock went nowhere, or worse, for three years; it was 50 in late 1996 and 50 in early 1999. But investors who didn't give up the ship were well rewarded. The cell phone business took off in 1999, aided by a greater-than-expected demand for wireless Internet access. The company's semiconductor operation was also booming. And when the AOL/Time Warner merger was announced in January 2000, investors figured Motorola's modem business would be a prime beneficiary. Analysts raised their estimates for 2001 and beyond. With everything going the company's way, the stock had moved all the way up to 180. As Dimitriades said, "That's what long-term investing is all about."

A visitor from another planet might not have been impressed. Long-term investing seems easy, if only because you don't have to do anything. More accurately, you have to avoid doing something—namely, selling in panic or disgust. But it's one thing to hold on if you're Rip van Winkle. It's quite another to retain your optimism when you're in the trenches every day the way Dimitriades was. Some points were due his way, even if he was fetching for them. The bunny rabbit was positively bug-eyed.

The bad news, which Cliff kept to himself, was that there wasn't really anything terribly special about Motorola relative to its wireless counterparts. You could have done even better if you owned Qualcomm, or maybe Ericsson or Nokia. Nokia was a Finnish company that happened to have the biggest market cap in all of Europe, having surpassed BP Amoco sometime during the cellular wave of 1999. But Cliff inferred that Dimitriades didn't own any of these other stocks, for the simple reason that he wasn't talking about them. Institutional investors are very selective conversationalists. But it also could have been professional rivalry creeping in. Cliff knew damn well that Qualcomm and Nokia were two of Kyle Hooperman's signature stocks. When Michael Jordan endorses Coke, Shaquille O'Neal endorses Pepsi. Such is the yin and yang of the spotlight.

The Gumbegone presentation didn't offer much new information, but Cliff sensed that most of the attendees were seeing the story for the first time. Unfortunately, lunch wasn't the best backdrop for this particular story. The sequence went as follows: chicken cordon bleu, video of gum sludge, tapioca pudding. But the novelty of the company seemed to hold the audience's interest.

The preliminary price talk centered on a range of $12 to $14 a share for an offering of 8 million shares. Those 8 million shares represented about one-third of the company, so the total market cap was in the neighborhood of $300 million, making it a pretty small offering. Not only was 8 million shares a fairly small number, but the number of shares actually available for trading—the so-called "float"—would be substantially less. Gumbegone investors weren't the sort of people who would quickly flip their shares after the offering—a practice that R&H was getting increasingly sick of. So most of the shares would be tied up for some time, and the limited float was likely to create a volatile stock.

The pricing of a new issue is a more delicate matter than most people realize. The goal of the underwriters is to determine a price that is a slight discount to the company's so-called aftermarket value, which is whatever price it is accorded when it actually begins to trade. In that way, the company is happy — it has its money — and investors are happy as well, which will of course help the underwriter's *next* offering. If the underwriters set the initial price too high relative to the company's earnings, investors could be turned off, maybe to the point of threatening the offering. On the other hand, setting the price too low is tantamount to throwing the client's money away. Complicating the process is the fact that most investment houses put in orders for much more than they really want, so that they will be left with a reasonable amount after the inevitable cutback.

Perhaps the greatest single irony of the whole game is that the biggest headlines are given to the IPOs that go up 500 percent on the first day of trading, even though you could argue that the underwriter totally missed the boat. No bonanza of that magnitude was expected with Gumbegone, but even the indicated price range would serve the company well. After coughing up the usual seven percent underwriting fee, there would still be a nest egg of $100 million with which to do things like pay off debt and build enough Gumbegone units to last the next quarter-century.

As the presentation was winding down, some pinstriped R&H wonk came to the podium to summarize the proceedings. He gleefully announced that there was strong demand for the offering, so he was confident that the deal would be fully subscribed. He reminded everyone of the "green shoe," which basically meant that the underwriters could buy up to 15 percent more shares during the first month of trading — at the offering price — in order to maintain a balance of buy orders and sell orders in the aftermarket.

"Why is it called a green shoe?" the bunny rabbit asked. He looked pleadingly at Dimitriades, who shrugged his shoulders. Cliff was more than happy to step in.

Cliff explained how the term came from a 1960 offering for a company called Green Shoe, which, in the '70s, took the name of its popular kids' brand—Stride Rite. When Green Shoe came public, the underwriters struck a deal with the company whereby they could purchase additional shares at the offering price after the stock was being freely traded. Those extra shares would help the underwriter manage the buying and selling of the stock in the aftermarket. It was the first deal of its kind, but it became a model for virtually every one that followed. It seemed fitting that you'd find mention of a green shoe in a red herring, but the truth was that one of the founders of Stride Rite was named Philip Green, who had long since left the company by the time it went public.

"So, you see, it really should be called the Slosberg shoe," Cliff said. The line always seemed to get a laugh.

The green shoe wasn't the only funny term floating around Salon Beaumont. The IPO circuit had a language all its own, and if you were an outsider it probably sounded like Esperanto. There was "collar," which meant the lowest offering price that would be acceptable to the offering company. There was "lock-up period," which referred to the fact that corporate insiders had to hold on to their shares for a specified period—typically, 180 days—before they could unload them. Day traders and other market vultures made a habit of tracking the IPOs that were reaching the 180-day mark, on the grounds that insider selling pressure could cause the stocks to weaken. The lock-up period was different from the "quiet period," the time following the offering during which underwriters and corporate executives are barred from saying anything material about the company's prospects.

When the presentation was over, Dimitriades folded his napkin and started to get up. This was the opportunity to detain him.

Cliff said, "So, do you think you'll end up buying shares?"

"If I were going to buy, I wouldn't tell you, now would I?"

Okay, so he wasn't tipping his hand. Managers seldom did. Skepticism looks much smarter than unbridled optimism in circumstances such as this, no matter what company happened to be selling its wares. But what rankled Cliff was the suggestion in Dimitriades's tone that Cliff was only there to get the master's opinion, upon which his own would be based. Cliff felt like challenging him to a quick game of Gumbegone Pursuit, but Dimitriades clearly wasn't going to give him the time.

"Well, I'm going to buy shares," Cliff said. "I think it's about a 70 percent shot, and that's plenty good enough odds for me." Slight pause. "You see, I'm an incurable optimist, maybe 'cause I'm a disciple of Kyle Hooperman."

"Who?"

CHAPTER 21

Wednesday began as a misty morning in Manhattan. There was a chill in the air. As Cliff looked out his living room window, he saw the early wave of Central Park joggers, most of them equipped with windbreakers and running gloves. But it didn't take more than a couple of hours for the city to warm up. By 10:00 A.M., the sun was piercing through Cliff's window and had made a bright rectangular patch on his living room floor.

Wednesday was also the day when a couple of old friends decided to check in.

Call number one came from Linda Greer, who sounded as if she had just run the Fifth Avenue Mile.

"Cliff, have I got a juicy little tidbit for you."

"I'm all ears," Cliff said, wondering to himself whether there was such a thing as a big tidbit. "But settle down. There's no hurry here."

"For you, maybe not. But Ginny just stomped off to the trading floor again."

"And you called me first? Linda, you know how jealous Geraldo gets."

"Let me finish," Linda said. "This time she isn't just squabbling over an eighth of a point here and a sixteenth of a point there, the way she usually does."

"Didn't know she was one of those," Cliff said. He was always amused by portfolio managers who called themselves long-term investors and then freaked out at the thought of overpaying by six cents per share.

"When it comes to getting executions on low-price stocks, she's cheaper than Kmart kitty litter, but that's not the point. A trade just showed up on her screen and she just blew up. I mean, I thought she was going to jump out the window."

"No such luck?"

"Cliff, it's 3-D Live. Seven of her clients now own it, at $5 per share."

Cliff stopped short. He had been maneuvering his fingers to make the shadow of a donkey inside the patch of sunshine, but now Linda had his full attention.

"The woman who swore that she'd never owned the stock and never would?"

"That's the one. You told me to call you if that ever changed. Well, it just did."

"So I guess now I have to go figure out what this all means."

"Beats working, doesn't it?"

"My thoughts exactly," Cliff said.

Cliff hung up the phone and walked around the living room like he was playing Hamlet. "Well, well, so Ginny has pulled a 180," he thought to himself. He went over to the breakfast table, where he had left his *Wall Street Journal*. He headed immediately for the price quotations for the American Exchange. There was good old TDL at $6½ a share. So whatever Ginny Truesdale was upset about, it surely wasn't timing. Her clients were probably the only 3-D Live shareholders in the free world who were now in the money.

Cliff had tried to keep up with the 3-D Live story, but it was a moving target. The company practically had its own daily column in the *Journal*, and the way things were going, it seemed guaranteed to be in the *Journal* at least one more time. That time would be in early April, when the paper did its customary review of the winners and losers of the first quarter. The very latest news, which was covered on page A3, was that the company's founding fools weren't going to last even that long.

Hubert Stanislaw had been sent packing by a special directors' meeting. The press release cited a "pattern of duplicity and over-promotion," which was a nice way of saying that he was a lying sack of shit. Of course, the departure didn't really qualify as news, because Stanislaw's ousting was as inevitable as *Austin Powers 3*. But to the stock market, seeing was finally believing. That's what explained the 1½-point move in the stock.

The unofficial term for that type of rebound was "dead cat bounce," which got its name from the notion that a dead cat will bounce if you drop it from a high enough altitude. Never mind that Isaac Newton would have disagreed. The idea behind the expression was that a single up day should not be mistaken for a sign of life. Even Boston Chicken shares had some good days in the months prior to the company's bankruptcy filing.

With 3-D Live, the good news was that, at $5 per share, the fluff in the stock was long gone. The company that remained was a mere shadow of Hubert Stanislaw's hype machine, but at least it was the part that had a prayer of profitability down the road.

To serve notice that the company was blazing a new trail, 3-D Live's interim chairman announced that its entire investment in its signature three-dimensional sports transmissions would be written off. This meant that 3-D Live's book value would go from $8 per share to just $2 per share at the stroke of the pen, but on Wall Street that's not always a bad thing. The more important message behind a write-off of that magnitude is that the company isn't going to throw any more money away while chasing a hopeless venture. If the book value had to go down as a result, well, you could say that it never was really worth what it appeared to be.

The third part of the announcement that caught Cliff's eye was that the company was introducing a product called the Power Sneaker, which it hoped to release by midyear. The product was basically a rewrapped form of the technologically valid portion of ActivEnergy. The problem with the ActivEnergy concept was that a normal human being wouldn't be able to generate enough electricity on a typical health club machine to make the whole exercise of capturing that energy worthwhile. The idea behind the Power Sneaker was that it could solve the problem of rechargeable portable computers by harnessing something called a piezoelectric conductor inside a special sneaker. The mere act of walking, while not generating an enormous output of energy, was still enough to power a computer. This was a product of great potential. Its major handicap was that it was made by a company with a credibility gap wider than Bryce Canyon.

Cliff's trance was broken by *Hawaii-Five-O* kicking in again. He didn't get to it until the third ring. This time, the voice at the other end was Dash Quillen's.

"So I guess you've heard the latest news out of R&H?"

"Dash, I was at Lenci's house 90 minutes after he was shot."

"Oh, not *that*. I didn't just hop off the turnip truck."

Dash was showing his age, Cliff thought silently. People didn't hop off turnip trucks anymore.

"So what's the *new* news?"

"Hughie Szabo is singing like a canary."

"Hallelujah," Cliff said to himself. Whatever Szabo was singing, it wasn't "Over the Rainbow."

"You remember those bad prices he gave for New York municipal bonds?" Dash asked.

"I can't say I've lost sleep over them," Cliff said. "But yeah, I remember."

"Well, Szabo is admitting that he skimmed clients' accounts. He says he and Hooperman ran the scam together."

Cliff said nothing for a few seconds. It was the way he got when immersed in thought, especially when he was thinking about what a putzhead he had been. Like now, for example. Because the sad truth was that, ever since Trace interviewed Lucky Sparks, there was enough information available to conclude that Hooperman and Szabo talked about more than the beauty of tax-free investing.

It was the damn Connecticut country club. Once Cliff got it in his head that Sparks lived in Connecticut, there was no reason to suppose any connection between him and New York municipal bonds. But obviously he lived in *New York*. Trace wouldn't have called their cars twins, or octuplets, or whatever, if their plates were different colors. The muni bonds that Hooperman bought for Sparks could have been handpicked by Hughie Szabo, felon-at-large.

As Cliff recalled, Sparks was pleased as punch that Hooperman had swapped him out of 10-year Treasuries and into muni bonds with the same maturity. On the surface, it was an attractive deal. Although his muni bonds yielded only 4.8 percent (less than the Treasury yield of 6.1 percent), for someone in the 39 percent tax bracket, a 4.8 percent yield was equivalent to a pretax yield of 7.9 percent—about two percentage points higher than the yield on his Treasury bonds.

The problem was that the actual spread should have been even higher, because Treasury bonds weren't nearly as good a deal as they had been in some prior years, relative to other fixed-income instruments. Their yields were on the low side, for a variety of reasons. There was the "flight to quality" factor that erupted in 1998, following an assortment of financial crises, ranging from the collapse of Far Eastern currencies to the Russian ruble, not to mention the fiasco and costly bailout of Long-Term Capital Management. There was also the fact that the U.S. Government was running a surplus, which meant that it wouldn't be issuing as many new bonds. When demand rises and supply dwindles, the only way for bond prices to go is higher, which in turn reduces the yield.

At the same time, municipal bond issuance was plentiful. Some observers felt that local governments were raising cash just so they wouldn't be caught in a pinch when Y2K rolled around. Whatever the reason, the surplus of muni bonds caused their yields to rise relative to Treasury bonds. The actual pretax spread between muni yields and Treasury yields in the fall of 1999 was more like 2.5 percentage points, not the 1.8-percentage-point spread that Lucky Sparks picked up. Hughie Szabo was able to offer a bad price for the bonds and still have it appear, to clients like Sparks, that the swap was in their interests. What made the scam work is that muni bonds are illiquid. They trade over-the-counter, which is to say that individual bondholders can't check on muni bond prices the way they can with stock prices. Lucky Sparks didn't even know what hit him. Unfortunately for Szabo, it looked as though some other clients did.

The stakes were considerable. That 0.7 percentage point in yield translated into over three points on the price of the bond. Skim that off of $5 million worth of bonds, and you've picked up over $150,000 for only one swap.

But Szabo couldn't have been scamming Hooperman, who had access to the actual prices. No, it was a two-man deal. They must have bought the bonds for their own account and then resold them.

"So Hooperman gave his clients lousy spreads, and he and Szabo pocketed the difference," Cliff finally said.

"Sure as shootin'," Dash said.

"Dash, can I assume that this would never have happened if you were still in charge."

"You got it," Dash said. "Blame it on the bossa nova."

■ ■ ■

Cliff didn't know quite what to make of the little nuggets that had come his way. The one thing that was certain was that Kyle Hooperman had stepped over the edge. It was also certain that Hooperman was dead. What wasn't so clear was how the two events might be related. And there was the matter of accounting for why the murderer kept going. Cliff tossed on a white cotton sweater and headed for Central Park.

Walking alone in Central Park during the middle of a workday had been one of Cliff's major adjustments upon leaving Rutherford & Hayes. He felt self-conscious in blue jeans and sneakers, but he wasn't about to put a suit on just to impress the other passersby. It took him a while to figure out that those other passersby weren't going to be impressed anyway. It took longer still to realize that they didn't even care what he did or didn't do. This was New York City, the city that doesn't sleep, the city where anything goes. If he did his best thinking while walking in the park, that's what he'd do.

Something was bothering him. Something that Hannah Diehl had said that didn't seem so important at the time. He absentmindedly hummed an old Bugs Bunny tune: "I'm looking over a three-leaf clover, that I overlooked be-three. . . ."

There wasn't much clover in Central Park on this March afternoon. A few crocuses, maybe, alongside the reservoir. But there was something that Cliff had overlooked. By the time he reached the east side of the park, the brainstorm had struck.

He ducked into the Guggenheim to use the phone. He was only a matter of blocks from the site of the Dutton murder, the one that started it all. Now things had come full circle. He called Trace's cell phone and prayed that he'd get an answer. Three rings later, she was there.

"You what?"

"I solved the case, that's what I said. I know who killed Kyle Hooperman."

"Tell me!"

"It's—"

"Wait," Trace said. "Don't tell me. I want to figure this out."

"Trace, I'm at a pay phone. I don't have the time."

"Yeah, well, I'm at Mainstage getting a hairy eyeball from the Class of 2001," Trace said.

Cliff said, "I'm calling because I want to meet with you tomorrow morning in the lobby of 777 Fulton. Ten o'clock. Can you make it?"

"On one condition."

"What's that?"

"That you at least tell me which facts you used. I've got 17 hours to piece them together." Trace fanned her hand as if to wave bye-bye to her colleagues. All she wanted was a few more seconds.

"We've had a lot of things to think about," Cliff said. "The perils of moneymaking scams. People owning stocks they said they wouldn't own. Other people owning stocks for a long time and getting filthy rich. The possibility that a man wore makeup to Hooperman's place. Train rides to Madison Square Garden. The circus in town. Corporate takeovers. People getting hosed on a bogus Internet IPO."

"Okay, okay, but your quarter's running out and so is my time. Which of these things played a role in your solution?"

"You won't believe it," Cliff said.

"Try me."

"All of them," Cliff said.

CHAPTER 22

When Cliff and Trace entered the lobby of 777 Fulton Street, even Nicky the Pinkerton's guy knew something was afoot.

"What's the occasion, Mr. Cavanaugh?"

Cliff was carrying two dozen balloons. Red ones, blue ones, yellow ones, even a few striped ones. "Just playing court jester for a day. Care to come along?"

"Nah, I'm on duty here."

"I'm not inviting you to a party," Cliff said. "I need you on official business. Enforcer business."

Nicky wasn't the brightest star in anyone's galaxy. He was only even money to tell you which river flowed past Croton-on-Hudson. But he could tell that Cliff was serious.

"I'll get someone to cover the lobby," he said.

Nicky returned in thirty seconds flat with a big grin on his face. Enforcement was his game. He stood six-feet-four, two hundred sixty pounds, with big, tree-trunk arms that could bench-press Linda Tripp. Yet, for most of his working hours, he functioned as an imposing but ultimately decorative lobby statue. This was his chance for some action. His fingers were getting twitchy around his billy club.

With Cliff, Trace, Nicky, and Cliff's miniature version of Macy's Thanksgiving Day parade, the elevator's real estate was spoken for. Suddenly the ride to the twenty-first floor was express. There was just enough time for Cliff to pay Trace an unexpected compliment.

"She what?" Trace exclaimed.

"You heard me. Ginny Truesdale has been buying some takeover candidates."

"What makes you so sure?"

"Linda told me, that's how," Cliff said. "She said Ginny's been scooping up insurance stocks and a few banking stocks."

"That snitch," Trace said.

"The worst kind," Cliff said. "And don't sit around waiting for any credit, either. According to Linda, Ginny sent out a client memo describing how, with the repeal of the Glass–Steagall Act, there's bound to be a consolidation in financial services. Plus the stocks are cheap after all the interest rate hikes of 1999 and early 2000."

Trace said, "And besides, a prospective client whom I haven't called back started me thinking along those lines."

"No chance of that," Cliff said. "You won't get any credit unless the idea blows up in her face." He started to say more, but was interrupted by the high-pitched ding of the elevator. It was show time.

"I'll do the talking," Cliff said as the doors opened. And Trace and Nicky were happy to nod in agreement. They weren't the ones with anything to say.

As Cliff had foreseen, the group's entry on 21 was aided by the magic of the balloons. Even in jaded Manhattan, balloons put smiles on peoples' faces. The receptionist waved them in without so much as a background check. She didn't even notice Nicky, which was pretty remarkable in and of itself, because Nicky was about as unnoticeable as Paul Bunyan and his blue ox. The threesome walked down the hallway toward the office of one Theodore D. Lenci. Hannah Diehl beamed when they reached her station. In the background, through the glass, they could see Dave Lenci at his desk. Funny thing, though. Lenci wasn't smiling.

Cliff went first.

"Hey there, Dave. Thought your office might need some cheering up."

"I'm going to call security," Lenci said.

"No need." Cliff stepped to the side, so the balloons were no longer impeding Lenci's view. Nicky seemed to appear out of nowhere, like one of Siegfried and Roy's white tigers. "You see, Dave, I've taken that precaution for you. Can we come in?"

Lenci didn't resist. He motioned for them to enter.

Cliff said, "Say, Dave, you don't mind if I tie these balloons down, do you? They're heavier than you'd think."

"I'll hold them," Nicky said, completely missing the point.

Cliff grabbed the "Theodore D. Lenci, Investment Counselor" sign from the desk. He pulled off a strip of Scotch tape from the nearby dispenser and attached the balloons to the nameplate. It didn't work. The balloons headed straight for the ceiling.

"Well, I'll be," Cliff said. "Did you see that, Dave? Did you see how the balloons pulled your nameplate straight up?"

"Cliff, I've been away for several days and I've got some work to do. Do you mind telling me what you're up to?"

"I just wanted to explain to my friends, Trace and Nicky here, how you managed to shoot yourself and make the gun go away."

"You can't be serious."

"Oh, but I am," Cliff said. "The aluminum version of the Colt Government Model weighs only fifteen ounces. Pocketlite, I think they call it. Did you realize that, Dave?"

Lenci didn't say a word.

Cliff said, "Oh, but of course you did. Silly me. You were carrying it that night, weren't you? You went to the circus in a separate car. You even let your wife drive your precious Jaguar just so the kids could have more fun. That was a nice touch, Dave. But the truth was that you needed the Suburban because it would fit a whole lot more balloons than the Jaguar ever could. You bought them as you left the circus. You tied them to the gun. You went and shot yourself and the gun went into the wild blue yonder. Except that you shot too close and nearly killed yourself in the process. You will stop me when I say something that didn't actually happen, won't you, Dave?"

"You can't prove a word of this," Lenci said. He said it through clenched teeth, like he was a guest villain on *Murder, She Wrote.*

Trace and Nicky were following the conversation like a ping-pong match, their pupils widening at every turn. But, true to the plan, they stayed as quiet as Shields and Yarnell.

"Oh, but maybe I can prove it," Cliff said. "Suppose I told you that a gun just washed up on the shores of Long Island Sound, tied to two dozen Ringling Brothers balloons?"

It was the world's oldest bluff, just like Ringling's being the greatest show on earth. But it seemed to work on folks who were seeing their life flash before your eyes.

"Look, I didn't kill Kyle Hooperman, if that's what you're driving at."

"Then why were your initials left on Hooperman's computer screen?" Cliff asked.

Lenci looked at the phone.

"Don't even think about it, Dave," Cliff said. "If you want to make a phone call, you can call your wife or your lawyer, that's it. Unless you want to call out for Chinese. You want Chinese for lunch, Nicky? Maybe some dim sum dumplings?"

Cliff looked back at Lenci. "Oh, how rude of me. Dave, this is Nicky. He'll be watching over you until the police show up. And this is Trace."

"Nice to see you again," Trace said. She waved her hand and as she waved you could see a flash of the Russian Roulette nail polish worn by Sandy Steinbach.

Not that Dave Lenci was noticing any nail polish.

"Look, I was double-crossed," Lenci shouted at the approximate volume of the R&H squawk box.

These particular words had a wider audience than he may have intended. By now there was a constant stream of spectators glancing into Lenci's office fishbowl. The scene reminded Cliff of the Fifth Avenue crowds that used to catch pieces of a Giants game through the picture window at Crazy Eddie's.

And the "double-crossed" part came through loud and clear.

"Double crossed, Dave? Those are pretty strong words. Suppose you tell us what you mean."

"You know damn well what I mean. Hooperman didn't leave my initials on his computer screen, *she* did."

"We'll get to her in a minute," Cliff said. "But does it occur to you that maybe Hooperman was just doing some research?"

"There's no chance of that," Lenci said. "Hooperman had already made his feelings about 3-D Live very well known. He said anyone owning the stock should be fired."

"Am I to suppose that you don't own the stock any more?"

"That's right."

"Suppose you check again," Cliff said.

Lenci's face was even more ashen than usual as he moved in front of his desktop machine to type out a few commands. The R&H portfolio tracking system, aka Big Brother, was set up to allow portfolio managers to survey their holdings any time they pleased. All they had to do was type in a ticker symbol and they'd see every client who owned a particular stock. If the stock wasn't held, the system would tell you so. But that's not what Big Brother was telling Lenci about 3-D Live. Cliff swiveled the monitor so that he and the rest of his troupe could see. One of Lenci's accounts owned 5,000 shares of 3-D Live, purchased at $5 a pop.

"I don't understand," Lenci said.

"What don't you understand, Dave? Looks to me like you're the proud owner of 5,000 shares."

"I sold all of my shares over a month ago. Something's wrong."

"Nothing's wrong, Dave," Cliff said. "Those shares were bought on Monday."

"I was in the hospital on Monday," Lenci said. "I wasn't taking fliers on any two-bit stock like 3-D Live."

"I never said you were," Cliff said. "Hooperman bought the shares, not you."

Lenci didn't say anything, but it was clear that the unicycles in his brain were working overtime. Cliff couldn't bear the thought of interrupting this historic event.

Lenci was coming around to what Cliff had pieced together the day before. It started with the fact that Hooperman had hated 3-D Live because he could see that its sales promotions were fraudulent and its revenue base was almost nonexistent. In his opinion, the stock didn't deserve to be anywhere near $59, $49, or even $28 per share.

But Hooperman wasn't the type to hold grudges—at least, not where investments were concerned. Cliff realized that what Hooperman must have done was to put in an order with the R&H floor trader to buy 3-D Live. But he didn't place a *market* order, which would have been executed immediately at the prevailing price. He must have asked specifically for a *limit* order, which told the broker to buy if the stock hit $5. If 3-D Live never collapsed to that level, the order would never be executed. And if it did hit $5, Hooperman's selected clients would be in.

Not that the stock couldn't go south from there. Panics are, by definition, unpredictable, and the $5 entry point was surely nothing more than an educated guess. However, it was a good guess. Once you looked beyond the write-offs, you could see that 3-D Live's power generation business had a viable future, either through its existing health club contracts or through its Power Sneaker. The whole point was that this part of the business had been all but neglected amid the excitement about 3-D imaging. Once the company invested more attention and money in power generation, they could easily earn fifty cents a share from the business—not bad for a $5 stock. And, under new management, 3-D Live still had some patents that could prove valuable—patents that the stock market was now basically giving away. It was a free shot, and it was working like a charm. The stock had gone from $5 to $8 in under a week, a 60 percent gain.

Dave Lenci was glum, and it wasn't hard to see why. Kyle Hooperman was deader than the macareña, but he was still outperforming the S&P 500.

And now it looked as though the wounds to Lenci's ribcage would be healing in the Big House. His own personal lockup period. And a quiet period, at that.

"Now suppose you tell everybody who double-crossed you," Cliff said.

Lenci said, "I'm calling my lawyer."

"Don't!" Cliff shouted.

Lenci reached for his phone anyway.

"Aaahhhhh!"

The salmon pranksters had struck again.

CHAPTER 23

The Four Seasons is one of New York City's most renowned gastronomic landmarks. Nestled in the Seagram Building on 52nd Street, it is cleverly within reach of every expense account on Madison Avenue. By day, it is the land of the three-martini lunch; by night it is the place to go if you want to be seen. At eight o'clock on the evening of March 22, the maître d' had a reservation for a party of two, under the name of Cavanaugh.

Cliff got there early, a poor calculation but understandable in someone whose adrenaline was five octanes up from rocket fuel. Murders don't get solved every day. Twin confessions are rarer still. And there was even more fun ahead. A multidigit check from Rutherford & Hayes promised to be sweet: The small print of the contract demanded that it be hand-delivered by Sean Cummings. And professional courtesy surely demanded placing a call to Jack Giardi. All these thoughts were dancing in Cliff's head as he stood next to the coat check station.

Whatever the reputation of the Four Seasons, it was a weird place. It had been designed by famed architect Philip Johnson, who, judging by the length of the corridor from the dining area to the men's room, had also designed Terminal C at Logan Airport. The dining room on the right, otherwise known as the Grill Room, was highlighted by large patches of walnut paneling. A bar in back was set underneath a sculpture of copper stalactites. Or maybe they were stalagmites. Cliff never could remember which pointed up and which pointed down. On the left side of the restaurant was Cliff and Trace's destination, the Pool Room, home to New York's largest un-used Jacuzzi. Both rooms had sky-high windows, and outside them were brass chains that hung like stage curtains, rippling in the wind. Between the windows and the art deco motif, the place had more glass and chrome than a Hyundai dealership.

Trace eventually appeared, and her entrance left Cliff shaking his head. If he were the one who was running late, he'd have arrived at five minutes after the hour in a full sweat. Instead, she prances in at quarter after the hour looking as unruffled as the model in an Estée Lauder ad. There was something to be said for her approach, and a lot to be said once she shed her black linen topcoat. Underneath was a purple dress with flowers made of black and red sequins, a skintight number that could have gotten her arrested in at least 43 states. The 75-year-old coat check guy was dumbstruck, and this was a man who two minutes before had been prattling about handling mink stoles for Ava Gardner.

The only thing that came close to spoiling Trace's entrance was her funched nose.

"I just don't get it," she said after dropping off her coat. "Why in the world would Lenci shoot himself if he wasn't the killer all along?"

"Because he's a yes man, that's why. He can be talked into just about anything if someone has the right carrot stick."

"So what's the carrot stick here?"

"For starters, a big chunk of Hooperman's client base."

"And for finishers?"

"Three hundred thousand shares of Intel," Cliff said. "He got 400 grand a year for doing absolutely nothing. That was the payoff."

"You're losing me," Trace said. "I thought Shari Beck was the Intel maven."

"She is indeed," Cliff said. "And she killed Kyle Hooperman."

"But—"

"No buts. She's already confessed."

Finally, Trace's nose straightened out and a bright smile emerged. "So it was a woman after all, was it?"

"Sort of," Cliff said. But the next voice wasn't his own.

"Good evening sir, madam. Will you come this way?"

Maître d' to the rescue.

Cliff got a kick out of seeing the heads that turned Trace's way, and then studied him, as they entered the Pool Room. She was the attraction, of course, and he had no problem with that, but society doesn't let a drop-dead redhead go by without at least checking out who's on her heels. Little did anyone know that he and Trace would be on the front page of *The Daily News*.

They ended up at one of the dozens of window seats that Philip Johnson had seen fit to provide. As they were being seated, Cliff couldn't shake the feeling that the scene was straight out of *Perry Mason*. After Perry solved a case, he and Della would find themselves either back at his office or at some swank L.A. bistro, the sole purpose being to tie up loose ends. Perry would explain how he got his hunches. They would laugh and revel in the smugness of victory. That's how they did it back in the '50s. But the Four Seasons was even better. It was real, it was now, and, best of all, there would be no goddamn Paul Drake to spoil the mood.

But Cliff had always wondered why the wrap-up conversation hadn't happened sooner. Okay, it was TV; but still, what were the producers thinking? Did Perry and Della take a cab from the courtroom to the office and not utter a single word to one another until it got dark? Did he taunt her with some sort of guessing game?

The guessing game angle worked on Trace, but only for so long.

"Okay," she said. "I give up. Why did she kill him?"

"You really want me to spill the beans?"

"As long as you remember that there's a big *but* surrounding this whole conclusion."

"I don't forget big buts," Cliff said. "The first thing you have to understand is that Shari Beck was blackmailing Hooperman into giving her top priority on IPOs."

"Sounds like a conjecture."

"Well, it started that way," Cliff said. "But so did Fermat's Last Theorem, and that one worked out okay."

"Wasn't it unproved for three centuries?"

"I can do better," Cliff said. "Remember how Hooperman scored big with McDonnell Douglas options?"

"It keeps coming up. Was it the only time he ever bought options or something like that?"

"Well, he bought Philip Morris options too, but that was as a hedge. The whole point was that he *didn't* dabble in options, and I don't think he would have bought an unhedged position in McDonnell options unless he knew damn well about the takeover."

"What does that have to do with Shari Beck?"

"Don't you see? McDonnell Douglas was bought out by Boeing. Shari Beck is on Boeing's board. She must have passed the word around to Hooperman. And once Hooperman acted on it, she blackmailed him."

"Insider trading."

"Exactly. Either he paid her off big time or she ended his career."

"But she was guilty too, wasn't she?"

"Not in the way he was," Cliff said. "The SEC doesn't care as much about loose lips as it does about actual profits. She'd only have a problem if she was a party to the insider trading. Besides, Hooperman couldn't rat on her without ratting on himself. And it really didn't cost him all that much. All he did was to give her preferential treatment on any Rutherford & Hayes IPO she was interested in."

"And she bailed out of URLybirds?"

"She sure did. The flip side of getting the securities you want is not getting the securities you don't want."

"Okay, but I always thought it was the blackmailer who got killed, not the blackmailee. What happened?"

"Hughie Szabo, that's what."

"He's connected to this?"

"Only in that he was hooked up with Kyle Hooperman. Once the muni bond scam was exposed, Hooperman's career was over. That's why he didn't bother taking the job at the Earhart Fund."

"You mean he knew he was through."

"Precisely. And once he was through, Shari Beck's trump card disappeared. Hooperman must have told her that he was going to go public with the IPO scam, because at that point he had nothing to lose. But she did have something to lose, because now she was in it up to her eyeballs just the way he was. So she snuffed him out, and she enlisted Lenci to shore up her alibi."

"But how do you know she enticed him with Intel shares?"

"Simple. The point is that even though Shari Beck owned enough Intel to buy out Leona Helmsley, she didn't place it under management with Hooperman. We know that because her account was worth $40,000 a year to Hooperman, about the same as all the other clients we looked at. That's a $4 million account. Peanuts."

"Yeah," Trace said, the way people say yeah when they're really thinking, "Prove it, buster."

"The thing I overlooked was Hannah Diehl telling me about the stock power she was processing. If clients already had their assets with Hooperman, their stocks would be registered in street name."

"Street name?"

"That's right. As far as the company is concerned, Rutherford & Hayes is the shareholder, not the individual client. So all the proxies and stuff get processed through R&H. There'd be no reason for a client to sign a stock power unless that client was handing over shares that were outside of R&H's existing holdings."

"Like Intel."

"Precisely. And with Intel in her managed portfolio, Shari could still get the first dibs on IPOs that she had gotten accustomed to, because her account would be ten times bigger. Only this time she'd be getting her treatment legitimately."

"But if Lenci was an accomplice, doesn't that imply that the two of them already knew each other even before he took over her portfolio?"

"I think the record will show that Lenci was handling her account while Hoop was shacked up at Betty Ford."

"The record will show?"

"Perry Mason talk," Cliff said. "But there's another clue. The way I have it mapped out is that Lenci told Shari Beck about 3-D Live while Hooperman was still ticking. So she goes to Hooperman with the idea, but he laughs in her face. He then embarrasses Lou Battaglia in that analyst meeting. So when Shari said that Lenci had mentioned the stock, it was sort of a slip of the tongue, but she didn't figure that the timing would ever come out, on account of the fact that Hooperman was dead. What she didn't factor in was that Hooperman would place that limit order on TDL."

"So how'd you know that he'd bought it for Shari Beck's account?"

"Linda Greer. When she told me that Ginny Truesdale owned the stock, at first I figured that Truesdale had just changed her mind. But she never seemed like the flexible type, at least, not compared to Hooperman. Kyle was the most flexible investor I've ever seen. And it dawned on me that he might have also bought it for clients that went on to Lenci instead of to Truesdale."

"Like Shari."

"Exactly. And remember, when a portfolio manager buys a stock, he buys it for all the accounts whose objectives it fits. The fact that she was the only one of Lenci's new clients to own it is sort of suspicious, though, isn't it? I mean, you might think that the same manager would inherit accounts with similar objectives. It's just another indication that maybe the decision that aligned Beck with Lenci wasn't pure chance. Besides, according to my previous conjecture, she had already mentioned 3-D Live to him. It all fits."

"So what put you on to Lenci?"

"The circus," Cliff said. "A guy like Lenci doesn't skip out on business hours just to see Ringling Brothers. Not when he could have seen them at Nassau Coliseum earlier in their tour and with a whole lot less hassle. And he certainly doesn't let a bunch of kids in his Jaguar after they've been pigging out on cotton candy. He had to have a reason. But the real tip-off was that he *drove* to Madison Square Garden. You just don't do that, not when the #2 line is a straight shot. But he had to do that, of course, because he had to take care of the balloons. The Suburban was perfect. It had all the space he needed, plus the windows were tinted for maximum secrecy."

Cliff stopped for a moment.

"You know, I gotta hand it to Lenci. The balloons were a pretty clever ploy, even if they weren't his idea. The murder weapon is disposed of, and any suspicion that had been placed on either of them goes away immediately. The fact that Lenci was such a dope that he almost killed himself made the whole thing even better."

"All right, Cliff, I hear you. But you were right there when Jack Giardi said specifically that Eric Beck took his mother out to dinner that night. They ate in *this* room."

"Correct on both counts," Cliff said.

"So how could she possibly have killed Kyle Hooperman?"

"Her alibi was only in our minds. Giardi never said that Shari Beck was having dinner with her son that night. He said that Eric Beck was having dinner with his mother."

"This is no time to play games, Cliffie."

"No games, I assure you. Do you happen to know when Intel went public?"

"Can't say as I do."

"October 13, 1971," Cliff said. "And she bought the shares as soon as she got out of college. You know what else?"

"What else?"

"As of that date, Princeton had yet to graduate a single woman. If 'Shari' graduated in 1971, she was a guy, plain and simple."

"So Shari Beck had a sex change operation?"

"That's what I'm saying. Shari Beck is Eric Beck's *father*."

"But I thought both parents went to Princeton."

"They did. Shari must have been older by a few years. When she/he graduated, the place was all male, but within a few years there were plenty of women undergraduates."

Cliff and Trace looked at one another and they knew precisely what was on the other's mind. There wasn't going to be any payout on their little side bet. Trace was going to claim that a woman was the murderer, and Cliff was going to claim it was a man. And neither side was going to give in.

Maurice the waiter returned to the table. He recited the specials of the day as if they were tattooed on the palms of his hands.

"And would you care for some wine this evening, Monsieur?"

Cliff shot a knowing glance Trace's way, then looked back at Maurice.

"We'll just have the usual."

"The usual, Monsieur?"

"That's right. Your very best Chateaubriand for two."